Sweet Fire

Tullia d'Aragona's
Poetry of Dialogue and Selected Prose

translated and edited by
Elizabeth A. Pallitto

George Braziller Publishers
New York

First published in the United States of America in 2006 by
George Braziller, Inc.

For further information, please address the publisher:

George Braziller, Inc.
171 Madison Avenue
New York, NY 10016

www.georgebraziller.com

Library of Congress Cataloging-in-Publication Data:
Aragona, Tullia d', ca. 1510–1556.
[Selections English & Italian]
Sweet fire : Tullia d'Aragona's poetry of dialogue and selected
prose / translated and edited by Elizabeth A. Pallitto. — 1st ed.
p. cm.
English and Italian.
Includes bibliographical references.
ISBN-13: 978-0-8076-1562-1 (pbk.)
ISBN-10: 0-8076-1562-5 (pbk.)
ISBN-13: 978-0-8076-1556-0 (hardback)
ISBN-10: 0-8076-1556-0 (hardback)
1. Aragona, Tullia d', ca. 1510–1556. 2. Poets, Italian — 16th
century — Biography. 3. Women poets, Italian — Biography. I. Pallitto,
Elizabeth A. II. Title.
PQ4562.A9A2 2007
851'.4 — dc22
2006022945

Designed by Rita Lascaro

Printed and bound in the United States of America

First edition

SWEET FIRE

CONTENTS

ACKNOWLEDGMENTS

Clare Carroll, my thesis advisor and mentor, has given me so much in the way of encouragement that my first thanks must go to her. An award-winning teacher and an exemplary model, her love of learning, teaching, and scholarship continues to inspire me. Infinite thanks to Electa Arenal, for being a mentor and an *exempla* in her pioneering work on Sor Juana Inés de la Cruz and in the fostering of women's studies.

I owe enormous thanks to the following Renaissance scholars and professors: Julia L. Hairston, Daniel Javitch, Ann Rosalind Jones, and Rinaldina Russell. Reviewing Rinaldina Russell's translation of Tullia d'Aragona's *Dialogue on the Infinity of Love* was not only a pleasure but also the beginning of this journey. Thanks to Ann Rosalind Jones for her generosity and for her trailblazing scholarship on Tullia d'Aragona. I wish to thank the "untold" scholars with whom I may not be personally acquainted but whose work has been invaluable to me (even if their work does not appear in my truncated bibliography): Fiora Bassanese, Rob Buranello, Virginia Cox, Konrad Eisenbichler, John Freccero, Ernesto Grassi, Paul F. Grendler, Victoria Kirkham, Constance Jordan, Maria Ornella Marotti, David Marsh, Deborah Parker, T. Anthony Perry, Guido Ruggiero, Erika Rummel, Deanna Shemek, Janet L. Smarr, Susanne Woods, and Domenico Zanrè.

Thanks to Jennifer Stone, who encouraged my nascent interest in Italian studies and steered me to the Comparative and Italian Literature program at CUNY Graduate Center. At Columbia University, I had the memorable and wonderful experience of reading Dante and Petrarch with Teo Barolini. At Hesperia Institute in Italy, I enjoyed Paolo Valesio's lectures on Cinquecento court culture, not knowing how relevant they would become to this project. My gratitude to my graduate and post-graduate CUNY mentors: André Aciman, Ottavio di Camillo, Peter Carravetta, William Coleman, Marty Elsky, Amy Mandelker; at Queens, to Tom Bird and Patricia J. O'Connor; to CUNY librarians Curtis Matthew, Alexandra de Luise, and Suzanna B. Simor. With gratitude to the memory of Dr. Charlotte Frick, Robert Dombroski, Fred J. Nichols, and Fred Purnell.

Special thanks for looking at the Italian and English versions of these translations go to the accomplished Renaissance men Luigi Bonaffini, Elio Montanari, and Justin Vitiello. Quite appropriately knighted in Italy for his literary and political work, Justin is not only an inspiration with his translations of poetry from the twelfth through the sixteenth centuries, but also a dear friend.

The librarians of the Biblioteca Nazionale Centrale di Firenze, the Folger Shakespeare Library, and the Rare Book Room of the New York Public Library have been indispensable to this project. Many thanks to the Jewish Foundation for the Education of Women (JFEW) for funding an idyllic year of research. At the Five Colleges Women's Studies Research Center: thanks to Amrita Basu, E. B. Lehman, Rick Griffiths, and my fellow "fellows," Susan Buchholz, Eva Martin Sartori, and Alev Cinar.

Thanks to Mary Taveras, my editor, whose acumen, patience, humor, and insight made this book's existence possible, and to George Braziller for his vision.

Thanks to the student midwives of this book: Leandra Cabrera, Filiz Dut, Tugce Fethan, Jodi Kaafarani, Gulay Önan, Aykun Özgen, Özge Sevim, and Duygu Ünlü. Thanks to my chair, Metin Boflnak, for helping me to balance teaching and research, and to my colleague Clyde R. Forsberg, Jr. for his hortatory guidance.

My infinite gratitude to my family, who made this book possible in many ways, not least of all with the gift of a computer on which to write it: Kathryn Motoviloff, Robert Pallitto, Ellen Motoviloff, Roger Miller, and Andy Miller. Many thanks to my accomplished siblings Rob Pallitto, John Motoviloff, and Christina Pallitto, for their love and support; likewise to my amazing "out-laws" and my wonderful *nipoti*.

I want to thank the following people for their friendship, sustaining humor, and intellectual provocation: Michelle Anderson-Cummings, Paul M. Bauer, Susan Bercaw, Ann Clarke, Heather L. Dubnick, Olga Guseva, Kathleen Kelly, Paula MacKenzie, Cyrus Moore, Justine Nicholas, Martin Paddio, Vittoria Repetto, and Berrak Yaflar.

For their specific contributions to this book, heartfelt thanks:

To Buket and Tayfun Aktas for the myriad ways in which they have helped me negotiate the confusing, if not Byzantine, intricacies of life in Turkey; in Tayfun's office to Gul, Tayfun, and Nurhan.

To Ben Alexander, historian, playwright, fellow traveler on the path of creativity; and to Susan Buchholz for introducing me to *The Artist's Way* and to Julia Cameron.

To Rebecca Curtis, for her intersubjective perspective and for believing in me. Thanks to Ihsan Gani Erbas, *kardesh* and guardian angel in Istanbul.

To Kevin J. McGinley for cat care, humor, and friendship.

To Bryan Gardner, who saw me through the first version of this book and the second, whose supportiveness and crisp British humor make life feasible and bearable.

To Michael Leibensperger, Renaissance patron of the arts.

To Elio Montanari for sharing with me his vision of the beautiful things of Istanbul and for enriching my own life via words, images, and ideas.

To Kadir Ozen, ideal reader.

To Román Santillán for help with countless research queries and in matters ranging from practical to arcane, for always being there for me. *Gracias.*

To Izel Sulam, last but not least, for his Jedi powers of computer wizardry.

To the memory of Anna Fryz Motoviloff and Donata Iacullo Pallitto.

PREFACE AND INTRODUCTION

The 2006 Bilingual Edition
(and previous versions) of the *Rime* of Tullia d'Aragona

The first edition of the *Rime della Signora Tullia di Aragona* was printed by the Venetian publisher Giolito in 1547, again in 1549 and in 1560; reprinted in Naples (1693);[1] in Bologna (1891); and the 1891 edition was reproduced in 1968.[2] Here, the order of the poems follows the 1547 edition.[3] Until now, the lack of an English edition of Tullia d'Aragona's *Rime* has deprived her of potential readers. To make matters worse, the nineteenth-century editor Enrico Celani not only changed the original punctuation, but also rearranged the poems. The electronic edition of the *Rime*, based upon the 1891 edition, falls prey to some rather heavy-handed editorial choices. Thus, the editions most available to scholars (the 1891 Bologna edition, its modern 1968 reprint, and the electronic version) continue to perpetuate incorrect versions of the text. By separating the originally intertwined exchange-poems, Enrico Celani distances Tullia d'Aragona from her network of fame. As Ann Rosalind Jones points out, this creates a melancholy portrait of a solitary poet rather than conjuring a vision of an admired member of a literary coterie.[4] This—and other misleading impressions of the poet—I attempt to rectify here.

Upon consulting the 1547 edition in the Biblioteca Nazionale Centrale di Firenze, I discovered how much the original had been altered, especially by Celani in 1891. The 1560 editor also made substantial changes, adding punctuation, adding inconsistent accent marks, and changing words that he felt might be erroneous. Tullia d'Aragona is a purposeful writer whose diction and linguistic choices carry subtle political and social meaning. For example, Tullia's linguistic choices (e.g., her use of the Spanish "donde" instead of the

Italian "dove") reflect an affinity with her Spanish patroness Eleonora de Toledo as well as her Aragón ancestry. In this book, accents have been omitted to more closely follow the original; missing letters, indicated by a *tilde* (~) in the original, have been added; and the original order of the poems has been restored.

Translator's Preface

> Ma bisognava che Madonna Laura avesse avuto a
> scrivere ella altretanto di lui quanto egli scrisse di
> lei, ed avreste veduto come fosse ita la bisogna.
>
> (Just think what would have happened if Madonna
> Laura had gotten around to writing as much about
> Petrarch as he did about her: you'd have seen things
> turn out quite differently then!)
> — "Tullia" in the *Dialogue on the Infinity of Love*
> by Tullia d'Aragona[5]

In the above quotation, Tullia d'Aragona imagines what it would be like to be Laura, Francesco Petrarca's beloved but mute Muse. We know that Laura has a face like an angel, blonde hair that floats in the breeze and ties the poet in knots, and a lovely hand that seizes the poet's heart from his breast—but we know nothing of her thoughts, even when the poet "gives" her words. Tullia, on the other hand, is an impassioned speaker. She is not only a muse, but she is also a vocal subject of desire.[6]

Because she attached such importance to her work, I wanted Tullia d'Aragona's distinct voice to come through in translation. Easier said than done: the alliteration and rhythm of the Italian does not always reemerge in the English, and other details are invariably lost. In the paired poems, for example, each response-poem uses the same rhymes as the originating sonnet, though I have not duplicated this feature in the English translation. I have, however, used slant rhyme to suggest the music of the original (as sonnets are, after all, "little songs").

It has been helpful to consider other translations of poetry whose work preserves the character of the original text: Robert Pinsky's translation of Dante's *Inferno*, with its solution of slant rhyme to suggest Dante's *terza rima* rhyme scheme; Justin Vitiello's daring (yet true to the original) English translations of Cinquecento Spanish and Italian poetry sonnets; Helen Vendler's detailed analyses in *The Art of Shakespeare's Sonnets*; and the translation of Sor Juana Inés de la Cruz's *La Respuesta* (The Answer) by Electa Arenal and Amanda Powell, which has served many writers as a model of translation and literary study. The introduction to *The Answer* combines rigorous scholarship with accessibility, and the book itself is a milestone in Latin American literature and gender studies. All of these interpretative strategies resonated with me as I strove to render Tullia d'Aragona's *Rime* into English—to cite just a few examples which have informed and inspired this project.

I respect the impulse of scholars who opt for prose translations, quite reasonably admitting the impossibility of the task of an accurate translation of poetry into poetry. Thus, my English translations of this Italian Renaissance poet will best serve readers as an impetus to further exploration: ideally, readers will be inspired to learn the language in which Tullia wrote and to improve upon my imperfect renderings.

For those who read Italian, it will be readily apparent that I have taken a certain amount of poetic license, inevitable in translation, in order to better capture the original. Paradoxically, by doing so, I hope to remain true to the poet I have come to know over the past nine years, to share her sorrows and triumphs with readers throughout the world.

On Translation

Introducing a sixteenth-century writer to a contemporary audience challenges one's conceptions of culture, language, and the very processes of linguistic signification. Translation not only occurs across languages but also in the transmission of thought from one mind to another. As John Locke said, we create "marks" and "sounds," to signify ideas, hoping to be understood.[7] Albeit imperfect—the need to communicate persists. Nothing has driven home this point more than my experience of living in Turkey. Most of my exchanges take place in translation; daily I find myself in situations from humorous to frustrating, but Turkish people have gone out of their way to be helpful and to transcend the language barrier. Perhaps living in Istanbul amidst centuries of history has given me the courage to complete this project: translating a writer's words and ideas from one time and place to another.

Introduction to the *Rime*

In poem XXVIII of her *Rime*, Tullia d'Aragona states her desire to be honored as a poet during her lifetime—and remembered after her death. To paraphrase a living writer, she was not just a courtesan who happened to write poetry, but a poet compelled "by necessity" to practice her mother's profession.[8] Tullia d'Aragona laments this misfortune in her epistle "To the Readers" (reproduced and translated in this volume). If she was indeed inducted into prostitution by her mother, Tullia's refusal to wear the courtesan's veil can be read as an act of resistance. Today, an educated woman with literary talent would not be constrained to practice prostitution as a profession—in theory, at least.[9]

Whatever the circumstances of Tullia's parentage and paternity, however, she received an unusually good education for her time. According to her biographers, Tullia d'Aragona received Latin instruction and could argue in that language.[10] Her singing and playing were said to be intoxicating and charming. Salvatore Bongi quotes a letter full of praise for Tullia's musical ability, her *excellentissima* knowledge, and her eloquence.[11]

The *Rime*, with its diverse display of poetic virtues, can give readers the means to decide for themselves. Not all of the poetry here is equal in literary merit, however. The first twelve poems are tributes to various members of the Medici family: in these sonnets,

Tullia lavishes praise upon her social superiors and eloquently praises other poets.[12] In the first section of the *Rime*, we get a glimpse of the courtierly persona that Tullia d'Aragona "fashioned."[13] In the poems to her, friends and fellow poets paint her in an admiring light as well—but when they venerate this latter-day Venus, they do so with great respect for her written work.

As the sonnet-exchanges demonstrate, Tullia's artist friends became her public supporters, most notably Girolamo Muzio (1496–1576). In the preface to his "Tirrhenia," Girolamo Muzio expresses a desire to be immortalized together with Tullia. He renames her as the muse Thalia, claiming that her love transports him to Helicon.[14] He also claims that he will outdo other poets, painting a portrait of her soul in words. Likewise, Tullia's poems merge the public with the private; display a range of emotions, settings, and occasions; and incorporate the imagery and rhetoric of Petrarch's poetry. They also contain allusions to classical myths.

Two of the most striking poems reference mythological figures from Ovid's *Metamorphoses*, one of the most popular printed books of the time.[15] In poem XXX, the speaker is Philomela, post-metamorphosis, a bird who escapes her "hated cage" only to be arrested by Love (Amor) and Virtue.[16] In poem XXXVI, the imagery of Psyche is used to sing the dark night of the soul.[17] Other poems contain learned arguments on theological and philosophical subjects such as "la questione della donna" (the woman question). In poem XXV to the radical preacher Bernardino Ochino, Tullia argues for free will, expressing sophisticated theological and literary arguments in sonnet form.[18] Poem XXVIII to Piero Manelli is a manifesto of gender equality and immortal fame.[19] The closing sestina sets an infinitely enduring love against a vision of apocalyptic darkness.

Clearly, the *Rime* were composed over time, not thrown together merely to obtain pardon for trangressing the sumptuary laws. Tullia d'Aragona was respected as a poet by the members of elite literary societies or academies, as well as by Cosimo I de' Medici, Duke of Florence and patron of the arts, and his consort Eleonora de Toledo.

The Life of the Poet

Tullia d'Aragona was born about 1510 in Rome, at the height of the city's wealth and the peak of its decadence. In the Eternal City, clergymen figured importantly in political, spiritual, and worldly matters. In addition to being the spiritual center of the Roman Catholic Church, Rome was also a thriving urban center of prostitution. It was known as the "city of women" because "celibate" male clergy were a prime market for the elite courtesans of the Cinquecento sex industry. Tullia's mother, Giulia Campana, was such a courtesan; her father, allegedly, was the Roman cardinal Luigi d'Aragona (1474–1519).[20]

Technically, the Church did not recognize children born to the clergy. In the case of the offspring of a courtesan, claims as to the child's paternity were even more suspect. The illegitimate sons of popes or cardinals, known euphemistically as *nipoti* (nephews), found positions within the Church nevertheless. Cardinal Luigi d'Aragona was himself an illegitimate son, the grandson of Ferdinand of Aragón (1452–1516). An illegitimate daughter like Tullia, however, had fewer options. Some accounts of Tullia d'Aragona's life, including fictional representations, claim that Cardinal Luigi was not Tullia's father; however, Giulia and the cardinal had a rather public relationship.[21] Whether or not he was Tullia's biological father, the cardinal seems to have been supportive while he was alive, contributing to young Tullia's education with financial support and to her humanistic education through his connections.[22]

As mentioned above, Tullia d'Aragona was said to be prodigiously intelligent, talented in dancing and music, known for her beautiful singing voice and her linguistic ability. Despite these advantages, however, the circumstances of Tullia's birth would determine her prospects, marital and otherwise. Although she claimed descent from the house of Aragón, a powerful dynasty whose members included the rulers of Spain and southern Italy, Tullia still could not expect to marry into the nobility. The Cardinal's relationship with Giulia had been public but not legal, thus leaving the courtesan and her daughter in a precarious financial position at his death in 1519.

As a young woman, Tullia helped support her mother and her "sister" Penelope, who was born in 1535. The large gap in age between them—about twenty-five years—leads some scholars to believe that Tullia might have actually been Penelope's mother.[23] The family relocated several times, living in Siena, Ferrara, Venice, and Florence, before finally moving to Rome in 1548. With the Counter-Reformation's increasing focus on public morality, laws became more stringent, and courtesans suffered legally and financially.

Penelope died in 1549, at age thirteen.[24] Critics have implied that the girl's death spared her from the necessity of entering the family profession, but Tullia, sensitive to the perils in which the circumstances of her own life had placed her, might well have tried to avoid imposing this fate upon Penelope. In the preface that introduces her chivalric epic, *Il Meschino Altramente detto il Guerrino*, entitled "To the Readers," (translated and included in this book), Tullia reflects upon her loss of innocence and laments "having had from [her] earliest years more knowledge of the world than [she] would wish to have had." Although this sentence can be read as penitential, such an admission suggests a certain discomfort with the "life" chosen for her by her own mother.[25] Tullia d'Aragona also pointedly states that *donne publiche* (prostitutes, literally, "public women") can fall into such a life through "bodily error" or the vicissitudes of fortune—not necessarily by choice. Sensitive to the stigma of her profession, she fashioned an alternative image for herself: with the publication of her *Rime* in 1547, Tullia d'Aragona achieved success and fame as a poet.

Friends and other supporters stood up in defense of the poet: over thirty authors comprise the *diversi* in the *Rime della Signora Tullia di Aragona et di diversi a lei* ("poems by Tullia and by others to her"); the "others" being poets, philosophers, and other men writing in praise of her character, talent, and intellect. The more well-known addressees in the "poetry of dialogue" include the poet-historian Benedetto Varchi and the esteemed man of letters Pietro Bembo. Tullia's friend Girolamo Muzio praises her royal lineage and her beauty, internal and external, in his sonnets and in his pastoral eclogue "La Tirrhenia" (written for Tullia and included in the *Rime*). Giulio Camillo and Benedetto Varchi pay homage to her soul in idealistic Neoplatonic language. The poet Benedetto Arrighi compares her, perhaps too favorably, to the noble Roman poet Vittoria Colonna (1492–1547): "It pleased the prime mover [God…] to adorn the earth, making Vittoria, a Moon and Tullia, a Sun" ("L'alto motor come 'l ciel ornar vole […] Far Vittoria una Luna, & Tullia un Sole").[26] The prestige of the poet-correspondents reflects well on the poet, as does the reciprocity and mutual respect evident in the *Rime*.

This dynamic of exchange and esteem from fellow poets also won the respect of the noble family, particularly Eleonora de Toledo. Tullia was declared permanently "free, exempt, and immune" from the sumptuary laws and allowed to dress as she pleased.[27] Acquiring cultural status through literary and philosophical works was a triumph for Tullia, who lacked many of the advantages that her contemporaries enjoyed. The accomplished poets Veronica Gambara (1485–1550) and Vittoria Colonna (mentioned above) were of aristocratic birth and had successful marriages.[28] With her Neoplatonic sonnets to her deceased husband, Colonna was an acceptable female Petrarchist and public figure.

While Gambara and Colonna were more socially respectable, they were less intellectually formidable, less provocative. Tullia d'Aragona, by contrast, challenged the received truths and cultural norms of her time. Perhaps as a courtesan/poet, Tullia could speak more freely: she refers to her "experience" in matters of love in her dialogue; expresses desire frankly in her poetry; and in the preface to her chivalric epic *Il Meschino altramente detto il Guerrino*, speaks to the social and literary conditions of women.[29]

In direct response to the woman question, or *questione della donna* that preceded feminism, Tullia d'Aragona addresses the idea of women as agents of their own desires. If reading and learning are made accessible to women, she claims, such pleasures will not abandon or disappoint them, unlike those fleeting pleasures that depend upon others, or upon means and circumstances. Tullia boasts that her epic in *ottava rima* verse will improve upon Boccaccio's prose work, responding to Boccaccio's claim, in the preface to his *Decameron*, that he writes for the "solace of women."[30] Indeed, *Il Meschino* is racy without being offensive, and Tullia presents her version as being more suitable for her potential audience of ideal readers that includes women.

The Poet as Defendant

In 1546, the Medici had been back in Florence for almost a decade. From the time Cosimo I took power in 1537 (followed by his marriage to Eleonora de Toledo in 1539), pomp and ceremony surrounded the court. Cosimo had enacted sumptuary laws requiring that courtesans wear a yellow veil to signify their profession, to distinguish themselves "from respectable ladies whose lives were honorable."[31] In Siena, Tullia d'Aragona had been threatened with fines for neglecting to wear the veil. Encouraged by Benedetto Varchi, she appealed as a supplicant to Don Pedro de Toledo. He in turn asked Eleonora, who interceded with Duke Cosimo on the poet's behalf.[32]

The author of numerous poems and a treatise on love,[33] Tullia d'Aragona was recognized for her intellectual talents by renowned poets and humanists who were willing to support her publicly. Thus, the category of courtesan did not entirely apply: Tullia d'Aragona chose to identify herself as an intellectual, a poet as well as a courtesan, and fashioned her image as such. Invested in his role as Duke of Florence and patron of the arts, Cosimo de' Medici recognized the substantial poetic talent of the defendant in this particular case. With a stroke of his pen he issued a pardon, writing on the legal document "Fasseli gratia per poetessa" (give her grace, for she is a poet). On the strength of her "rare knowledge of poetry and philosophy"[34]—and with the help of her patrons—Tullia d'Aragona's image underwent a change, from *cortigiana* (courtesan) to *cortigiano* (courtier) who used her poetic skills to bring honor to herself and to the Medici court.

The Poet as Courtier, or the Yellow Veil and the Laurel: Tullia d'Aragona's Florentine Sojourn (1545–48)

It is important to establish the relationship between the publication of Tullia d'Aragona's 1547 *Rime* and Cosimo de' Medici's pardon of the poet for her breach of his sumptuary laws. The 1547 *Rime* have been described as "a thank-you offering for the exemption."[35] Indeed, the dedication and the first fourteen poems (out of the thirty-eight poems by Tullia in the first section of the *Rime*) are tributes to members of the Medici family, but many of the poems predate both the affair of the veil *and* the publication of the *Rime*. Tullia d'Aragona also had prior connections within Florentine literary circles. Thus, the fact that the poems were published "on the heels of the exemption"[36] should not lead one to conclude that Tullia d'Aragona's poetry was occasional, ghostwritten, or lacking in substance. She was not a courtesan masquerading as a writer to avoid the law and gain sartorial freedom, but a writer who played a significant role in the Florentine cultural world of Cosimo de' Medici.

In recently published work, Deana Basile and Domenico Zanrè concur on Tullia d'Aragona's place in the official culture of the Florentine Medici court. According to Basile, "d'Aragona's sojourn in the city undoubtedly represents the most productive and successful period of her career."[37] To be a writer in one of the most artistically prominent Renaissance court cities also carried political significance: Tullia d'Aragona, Benedetto Varchi, and the poet-painter Agnolo Bronzino enriched the cultural program of the reestablished Medici regime. In the tenuous political climate in which Cosimo came to power, image-making provided essential political as well as cultural capital.

When Cosimo de' Medici decided to grant Tullia d'Aragona clemency for her breach of the sumptuary laws, he was demonstrating his ability to rise above the letter of his own law. Supporting poets who wrote in the Tuscan dialect was also a shrewd way to promote civic pride. While the choice of dialect might not seem particularly earth-shattering today, *la questione della lingua* (language question) was a major issue of the day; as a result, the standard Italian of today is closely related to the "Florentine" dialect.

In an effort to underscore the centrality of Florentine culture, some members of the Accademia Fiorentina went to far as to spread theories that Tuscany was founded by Noah himself, that the Etruscans (Florentines) were his descendants, and that Tuscan was linguistically descended from Hebrew and from Aramaic, the language spoken by Jesus.[38] Cosimo de' Medici welcomed pro-Florentine propaganda and even encouraged it, albeit passively. These theories divided the Accademia Fiorentina, and the "Etruschi" and "Aramei" factions were born. When Tullia's friends Ugolino Martelli and Benedetto Varchi scoffed at claims of Tuscan's Biblical origins, they in turn became the target of attacks.

> La Tullia, il Varchi, ed Ugolino e lei
> Hanno fatto lega, e studian tutta la notte
> E voglion pur che i ranocchi sian botte
> E che gli etruschi non siano aramei.

> Tullia, Varchi, Ugolino, and another [woman]
> poet have formed a league, where they study
> all night, and they claim that frogs are toads
> and that the Etruscans are not Aramaic.[39]

As Domenico Zanrè writes, "Tullia's affinity with Florence's *literati* was apparent in her friendships with those who had been part of the original Accademia degli Umidi, as well as with the members of its successor, the Accademia Fiorentina." [40] Dissension in the ranks of the official Academy worked to d'Aragona's advantage. When the original members found themselves embroiled in controversy, they met informally at Tullia's apartments, "a comfortable and perhaps more welcome alternative setting [...] frequented by Ugolino Martelli, Lattanzio Benucci, Simone Porzio, and Ridolfo Baglioni." Don Luigi and Don Pedro de Toledo also "honored the salon with their presence."[41]

Perhaps an inverse relation exists between the less glamorous realities of the life of a courtesan and the lofty heights of the *Rime*. In disfavor with the officially-sanctioned culture of the Medici regime, some of the writers of Tullia's salon created an academy outside the Academy. The salon is depicted in Sperone Speroni's 1542 *Dialoghi d'amore* (written in 1537 and published in 1542), as a fictional conversation between Tullia and the poet Bernardo Tasso, in which Tullia is depicted as more of a lover of the male poet than a poet herself.[42] Responding to Speroni's depiction of her, Tullia d'Aragona wrote herself as the character "Tullia" in her own 1547 *Dialogo...della infinità di amore*.[43] Her *Dialogue on the Infinity of Love* is a unique philosophical treatise in which "Tullia" has much to say on the subject, given her "experience" in matters of love. Also in 1547, with her *Rime della Signora Tullia d'Aragona et di diversi a lei* (Poetry by Signora Tullia d'Aragona and by others to her), she made her mark in a traditionally male realm: the elite world of Petrarchan poetry.[44]

L'Erodiade, or A Portrait of the Artist as Salome: Biblical Iconography, Biographical Evidence, and Speculation

Some scholars believe that the painting reproduced on the cover of this book is a portrait of Tullia d'Aragona, although others express doubt as to whether this is the case.[45] The artist is Moretto da Brescia, also known as "Il Moretto," and the painting is currently located in the Pinacoteca Tosio-Martinengo in Brescia, Italy. Restored in 1986 under the direction of Giuliano Casella, some of the work's original chromatic brillance has been recuperated. Art historians have commented that the work's "Raphaelesque grace wedded to the vigorous Venetian *colorire* adds enchantment to the beautiful face."[46] The image is 56 x 39 centimeters in size, the medium is oil on canvas, and a Latin inscription, incorporated within the painting itself, reads: QUAE SACRU[M] IOANNIS CAPUT SALTANDO OBTINUIT (she who obtained the head of John [the Baptist] by her dancing). At one point the painting belonged to a convent; then in 1829 it was bought by the collector Tosio Martinengo. Tullia's nineteenth-century biographer Guido Biagi claims that the inscription was a Biblical reference added at the request of the nuns.[47] If *L'Erodiade* is indeed a portrait of Tullia, however, the reference to Salome may refer to events in Tullia d'Aragona's life, such as the polemic with her contemporary Bernardino Ochino, the preacher.

In his book *Alessandro Bonvicino, il Moretto*, Pier Virgilio Begni Redona comments:

> [O]ne sees in (Salome), who is presented with the sceptre of a queen, separated from the macabre field of action, against a background of laurels: not the dancer, but a young woman with little liveliness; not the tragic carrier of the severed head, but a princess [literally, little queen] of the *commedia*, whom no one would recognize if not for the fact that she was leaning against the marble [parapet] with the inscription declaring her identity.[48]

This portrait is typical of works by Il Moretto: a figure of delicate melancholy, sumptuously attired.

The subject matter and the inscription are typical of the period. In the Renaissance, it was not unusual for an artist to select a saint or legendary figure to represent an actual person; the Biblical characters Salome and Judith were popular subjects of Cinquecento paintings.[49] A more interesting question would be, why was Tullia d'Aragona depicted as Salome? As is the case with other unresolved questions regarding her biography, the researcher must gather evidence useful in reconstructing the life of the poet. Perhaps this painting can shed light upon the limited information we have on this interesting Renaissance woman. If the image is a portrait of Tullia, it certainly reflects her regal bearing, her noble lineage, her status as a poet, and her expressive countenance. The delicate features and facial expression could be said to correspond to the precise and melancholy beauty found in Tullia d'Aragona's *Rime*.

At any rate, the painting was exhibited as a portrait of Tullia d'Aragona in 1823, along with a poem mentioning the scepter and the laurel, references to her noble—albeit illegitimate—ancestry. If her father was indeed Cardinal Luigi d'Aragona, or even Pietro Tagliavia d'Aragona, the archbishop of Florence and another of Giulia's patrons, Tulla is indeed a descendant of the house of Aragon. The flattering iconography is verbally echoed in a poem by Muzio Iustinapolitano, included here among the translations of Tullia's *Rime*.

The physical description of Tullia d'Aragona, not considered beautiful by the standards of her day, is consistent with *L'Erodiade*. Some of this negative bias may originate with Giambattista Giraldi Cinthio, possibly a spurned admirer. Cinthio considered her too tall and thin, with lips that were too full and a nose that was too long. Giraldi does admit, however, that her mischievous eyes (*occhi ladri*, literally "felonious eyes") sparked fire in the heart of anyone who gazed into them. The portrait, however, seems to reflect the poet in a more serious mood. The subject of the painting is an appropriately subdued and serious poetic figure, with laurels as background foliage, and royal dress indicating her station.[50]

The portrait's details include both classical iconography—laurel leaves, an appropriate symbol for a Petrarchan poet—and contemporary references to the poet's ancestry. The scepter held by the young woman in the painting is thought to represent Tullia's noble lineage; the figure is attired in garments traditionally suggestive of royalty, such as the ermine stole. Her hair is also adorned with pearls, a fashion explicitly mentioned in the Florentine sumptuary laws of 1546. Such adornment, adapted from the so-called "Orient," was popular in Cinquecento Italy. Ann Rosalind Jones describes the striped veil as "a textile signifying the Middle East." Of course, fashions travelled from Constantinople to Venice and other Italian court cities. The imaginative literature of the Renaissance, such as the chivalric epic, exhibits a fascination with the dress, customs, and mores of the oriental Other.[51]

The painting is known as *L'Erodiade* after Herodias, the mother of Salome. According to the Biblical account, Salome's dancing so pleased King Herod that he offered to grant whatever request she made. At a loss, The young Salome went to her mother, who immediately suggested that she request the head of John the Baptist on a platter. Herod, having given his word, complied.[52] Whoever might have corresponded to John the Baptist in the life of Tullia d'Aragona remains a mystery, although the preacher Bernardino Ochino resembles the radical New Testament figure. In poem XXV, Tullia addresses him directly. Ochino's extreme views on such sinful behavior as masquerades, dancing, and music would correspond to the strict morality of John the Baptist. Drawing a parallel between John the Baptist and Bernardino Ochino would create a sensational connection between Tullia and Herodias — and the grisly tale of Salome.

Tensions between the strict morality of early Christianity and the amoral court of Herod make an interesting parallel with the subject of the painting: Bernardino Ochino would be seen as fanatical in contrast to the worldly Florentine court of Cosimo de' Medici. Although Ochino was active after the death of Savonarola in 1498, he encountered resistance to his extreme views, as did his earlier counterpart. Tullia's biographer Enrico Celani speaks of "the harsh and menacing tone of the voice of San Bernardino [and] Savonarola."[53] Both men called for repentance in tones reminiscent of John the Baptist. The woman in the portrait may not represent the vindictive Herodias but rather the young girl who is caught up in a difficult political situation, much like Tullia.

Situated in the context of then-contemporary quarrels over theology, Tullia d'Aragona's opposition to Bernardino Ochino appears to be intellectual and theological. If she did have some personal quarrel with him, however, it would further explain the boldness of her argument. Theologically, most Florentines would have been opposed to such puritanical proscriptions. Furthermore, implicit in the language of the last line of the first stanza, *opre sante eterne* (eternal holy works) is the controversy over salvation by faith or by works.

BERNARDO, ben potea bastarvi haverne
Co'l dolce dir, ch'a voi natura infonde,
Quì dove 'l Re de' fiumi ha piu chiare onde,
Acceso i cuori a le sante opre eterne.

Che se pur sono in voi pur l'interne
Voglie, e la vita al vestir corrisponde,
Non huom di frale carne, & d'ossa immonde,
Ma sete un voi de le schiere superne.

Hor le finte apparenze, e 'l ballo, e 'l suono
Chiesti dal tempo, & da l'antica usanza
A che così da voi vietati sono?

Non fora santità, fora arroganza
Torre il libero arbitrio, il maggior dono,
Che Dio ne diè ne la primiera stanza.

BERNARDO, it should have been enough for you —
with your sweet speech by nature infused,
here by the famous waters of the king of rivers —
to set hearts aflame to deeds holy and true.

And yet, if your desires are pure within
if your inner life matches your outer robes,
you are not a man of worldly flesh and bone
but from the highest ranks of seraphim.

Costumes, masquerades, and music sweetly played,
sanctioned by use and by custom honored still —
why do you prohibit these ancient pastimes?

It is not holiness, but arrogance displayed
to take away the greatest gift — free will —
bestowed by God from the beginning of time.

The rhetorical structure of the poem bears noting. In the first two
stanze, Tullia d'Aragona appears to praise Ochino, but her praise is

qualified, conditional: *if* your pure desires are met, and *if* your inner life is consistent with your outer robes, *then* you must be exempt from the flesh entirely, like one from the ranks of seraphim. Of course, an ironic tone underlies the rather large *if*: can he (or anyone) make the claim of acting in a manner wholly consistent with his stated beliefs? Using Ochino's own proto-Calvinist argument against him, d'Aragona emphasizes the goodness that springs from inner faith as opposed to that which is imposed from external prohibitions—by means of rhetorical antithesis and paradox.[54]

Theologically speaking, moreover, there is an implied element of doctrinal controversy in Ochino's thinking: if one accepts the doctrine of the incarnation of Jesus in human form, then to claim exemption from the same temptations he experienced would be to commit the heresy of denying the dual nature of Christ. Ochino seems self-righteous: indeed, led by his reformist zeal, he is missing a more important spiritual and doctrinal point. He can serve God by inspiring others to holy works by his example, but also by allowing less-enlightened beings the dignity of free will. By saying it is not holiness but arrogance, Tullia is criticizing Ochino's spiritual pride as potentially more sinful than the harmless and time-honored pastimes of masquerades and dancing. His real sin, however, is to play God: to take away the free will that God has given us from the beginning (literally, "in the first place").

Tullia d'Aragona's sonnet to Ochino is an ingenious theological argument in favor of free will, a doctrinal quarrel which later becomes a major point of contention between Catholic and Protestant theology. While Ochino wants to prohibit sinful behavior and promote holiness by outwardly controlling popular forms of entertainment, Tullia d'Aragona's poem argues for the free will of the individual. Furthermore, she sees free will as a great gift from God, who allows human beings to choose to worship Him.

Poetically, Tullia d'Aragona's language is reminiscent of Dante's *Purgatorio* in the depiction of Virgil's last speech to Dante-pilgrim (XXVIII.140). About to deliver Dante into the care of Beatrice, Virgil grants that the pilgrim has earned the right to graduate from his master's tutelage into his own free, correct, and wholesome will: "libero, dritto e sano tuo arbitrio." While the pilgrim's independence is hard-earned after his journey through Inferno and Purgatorio, he has acquired the judgment to choose for himself. By echoing these lines of Dante, d'Aragona claims authority, both artistic and theological, for own views.

In her poetry as well as in the prose of her dialogue, d'Aragona is quick to point out inconsistencies in her opponents' arguments. The hypocritical behavior of men of the clergy, which would have been apparent to any *cortigiano* (courtier), must have been even more strikingly ironic to the *cortigiana* Tullia, as she herself was most likely the product of an illegitimate union between a high-ranking cardinal and a Roman courtesan.

As for Bernardino Ochino, his beliefs created major difficulties in his life. He was persecuted by the Inquisition in Florence, and forced to flee Italy for Switzerland and England. In Geneva, he met John Calvin and converted to Calvinism. For some time, Ochino preached in England and Zurich; eventually, however, he was also rejected by the Calvinists.

Although he was not literally beheaded like John the Baptist, Ochino did lose the right to preach in Florence. To add yet another dimension to this interesting historical puzzle, Tullia's faithful friend and admirer Muzio wrote a prose tract against Ochino entitled *Mentite Ochiniane* (Ochinian Lies).[55]

Perhaps Tullia d'Aragona's *Rime* contributed to Bernardino's fall—or perhaps his own outspoken beliefs and extreme views caused him to run afoul of the Inquisition and alienate the powerful religious and secular leaders of Florence. In either case, the victory goes to the Cinquecento Salome, symbolic beheader of a contemporary John the Baptist figure, the preacher Bernardino Ochino.

THE POETRY OF TULLIA D'ARAGONA
FROM *LE RIME DELLA*
SIGNORA TULLIA DI ARAGONA...

To the most illustrious and excellent Lady the Noble
Signora Eleonora di Toledo[1] Duchess of Florence,
her most respected patron, from Tullia d'Aragona

Most noble and virtuous Lady Duchess, in my humble condition I know very well how my poetic compositions, unworthy of Your Excellency with their unpolished roughness, are beneath her in wit and in judgment. For this reason, I was long in doubt as to whether I should address, to so great and honored a name as that of your Excellency, such a relatively trifling and ignoble labor as these Sonnets, often composed by me in order to escape *otium,*[2] or to refrain from seeming discourteous to those who had guided me — not only because I believed that it was necessary to be prized or that I should acquire value in the eyes of others, but I also desired to show, at least in part, my devoted servitude toward Your Excellency because of the many and great debts that I owe to her, and to her most glorious Consort.[3] Finally, taking these ardent tasks to heart, I resolved not to be lacking or delinquent to myself, reminding myself that the compositions of all writers, in every language, especially those of Poets, have always had such grace and preeminence, that no one, however great, has ever refused them, but everyone has always cherished them, and held them most dear.[4] For, as I know very well, despite the height of her state, and the humble stature of my condition, I present humbly and with most devoted heart this tribute of my few, small, base, humble labors to one of many, great, and most high virtues, with all my soul beseeching her to look not to the gift or to the giver, but to look to herself, with the highest regard.[5]

I *Allo Eccellente Signore Duca di Firenze*

Se gli antichi pastor di rose, & fiori
Sparsero i tempii, & vaporar gli altari
D'incenso a Pan, sol perche dolci, & cari
Havea fatto a le Ninfe i loro amori,

Quai fior degg'io Signor, quai deggio odori
Sparger al nome vostro, che sian pari
A i merti vostri, & tante, & così rari,
Ch'ognihor spargete in me gratie, & favori?

Nessun per certo tempio, altare, o dono
Trovar si può di così gran valore,
Ch'a vostra alta bontà sia pregio eguale.

Sia dunque il petto vostro, u tutte sono
Le virtù, tempio; altare, il saggio core,
Vittima, l'alma mia, se tanto vale.

II

Signor pregio, & honor di questa etade,
Cui tutte le virtù compagne fersi,
Che con tante bell'opre, & si diversi
Effetti gite al ciel per mille strade;

Quai sien, che possan mai tante, & si rade
Doti vostre cantar prose, ne versi?
In voi solo (et son parca) puo vedersi
Giunta a sommo valor somma bontade,

Voi saggio, voi clemente, voi cortese;
Onde nel primo fior de'piu verd'anni
Vi fu dato da Dio si grande impero,

Per ristorar tutti gli andati danni,
Et con potere eguale al bel pensero
Por sempiterno fine a tante offese.

I   *To the Excellent Signor Duke of Florence* [6]

If the shepherds of old with roses and flowers
scattered the temples and perfumed the altars
with incense to Pan, [7] who made them sweet and dear
to the favored nymphs, their lovers,

what flowers should I scatter, what incense diffuse
in your name, that may compare
with your virtues, so many and so rare
that with favor and grace I am ever infused?

Surely no one could find temple, gift, or altar
of such immense worth as to be on par
with your high bounty, your great valor.

Let your breast, then, be a temple, the living
seat of all the virtues; an altar, the wise heart;
an offering, my soul—if it is worthy of giving. [8]

II

Signor, the matchless jewel and honor of this age,
one with whom all the Virtues converse:
The report of your works, so noble and diverse,
goes skyrocketing to heaven by a thousand ways.

How could one pay tribute, in prose or poetry,
to all your gifts, so diverse and so rare?
In you alone one sees (and I cannot say more)
joined with the highest valor, the highest bounty.

So wise are you, so merciful, so courteous
that in the first flower of your greenest years
God has given you this great empire [9]

to remedy past evils and put—
with power equal to high thought—
an everlasting end to the ills that burden us.

III

Signor d'ogni valor piu d'altro adorno;
Duce fra tutti i Duci altero, & solo:
COSMO, di cui da l'uno a l'altro polo
Et donde parte, & donde torna il giorno

Non vede pari il Sol girando intorno,
Me, che quanto piu so v'onoro, & colo,
Prendete in grado, & scemate il gran duolo
De l'altrui ingiusto oltraggio, e indegno scorno.

Ne vi dispiaccia, che'l mio oscuro, & vile
Cantar cerchi talhor d'acquistar fama
A voi piu ch'altro chiaro, & piu gentile;

Non guardate Signor, quanto lo stile
Vi toglie (ohime) ma quel che darvi brama
Il cor, ch'a vostra altezza inchina humile.

IV

Nuovo Numa Thoscan, che le chiar'onde
Del tuo bel fiume inalzi a quegli honori,
C'hebbe gia il Tebro; e le stelle migliori
Girano tutte al gran valor seconde;

Le tue virtuti a null'altre seconde
Alto suggetto a i piu famosi cori,
Da l'Arbia, ond'hoggi ogni bell'alma è fuori,
Mi trasser d'Arno a le felici sponde.

Et al primo disio nuovo disire,
M'accende ogn'hor la tua bontà natia:
Tal che miglior non spero, o bramo albergo.

Così potessi un di farmi sentire
Cortese no, ma grata con la mia
Zampogna, ch'a te sol, bench'indegna, ergo.

III

Signor, adorned with valor more than any other,
leader among leaders, proud and alone,
COSIMO, a cosmos, from one pole to another,[10]
from where the day begins to where it must return:

The orbiting sun has not seen your equal born,
and as for me, how I honor and cultivate
one who lessens others' sorrows: such great
unjust outrage and unworthy scorn.

May it be pleasing, my rude and humble
song, but as you are seeking fame that endures,
Signor, most renowned and noblest by far,

do not regard, alas, how much my style
detracts, but look at that which you desire,
and humbly inclines to your height, my heart.

IV

New Tuscan Numa,[11] may the bright waters
of your lovely river be raised to the honors
the Tiber once held, and may the better stars
revolve in the orbit of your great valor.

Your virtues are second to no other,
the lofty subject of the most renowned choirs.
From the Arbia, where every beautiful soul goes forth,
I am drawn to the Arno's felicitous shores.[12]

And to a new desire, my first desire gives place,
your innate bounty filling me with light:
I do not hope or long for a better resting place.

Thus I hope one day to feel at ease —
court-worthy, no, but welcome for my flute,
which I raise to you, undeserving of your grace.[13]

V

Signor, che con pietate alta, & consiglio
(Onde tanto piu ch'altro al mondo vali)
Venisti a medicar gli antichi mali
Del fiorito per te purpureo giglio;

Io che scampata da crudele artiglio
Provo gli acerbi, e ingiuriosi strali
Quanto sian di fortuna aspri, e mortali,
A te rifuggio in sì grave periglio;

Et solo chieggio humil, che come l'alma
Secura vive homai ne la tua corte
Da la vicina, & minacciata morte,

Così la tua mercè di ben n'apporte
Tanto, che l'altra mia povera salma
Libera venga per le ricche porte.

VI

Dive, che dal bel monte d'Helicona
Discendete sovente a far soggiorno
Fra queste rive; onde è che d'ogn'intorno
Il gran nome Thoscan piu altero sona,

D'eterni fior tessete una corona
A lui, che di virtù fa'l mondo adorno
Sceso col fortunato Capricorno,
Per cui l'antico vitio n'abbandona.

Et per me lodi, & per me gratia a lui
Rendete o Dive, che lingua mortale
Verso immortal virtù s'affanna indarno;

Quest'è valor, quest'è suggetto tale,
Che solo è da voi sole, & non d'altrui,
Così dicea la Tullia in riva d'Arno.

V

Signor, whose grave counsel and high piety
make you most worthy to govern Florence
and to heal the ancient ills of the lily[14]
flowering, in royal purple resplendent;

Having escaped Fortune's claws so cruel,
I still feel her bitter crippling blows,
as harsh and mortal as she allows,
and flee to you for refuge in grave peril.

And I humbly ask that as my soul
lives secure, so let me ever live in your court,
safe from death's close and menacing fate.

Thus your life-bringing mercy makes me whole,
so that my other self, my poor corpse,
may enter freely though the richest gates.

VI

Goddesses, who from the lovely mount of Helicon[15]
deign to descend in frequent sojourn
along the Arno's banks,[16] which resound
with the great Tuscan name's proud sound:

Of ageless flowers weave for him a crown,
the one whose virtues the world adorn;
born under fortunate Capricorn,[17]
through him ancient vice is disallowed.

And through me praise, through me give thanks
to him, O Muses, that as my mortal tongue labors
toward immortal virtue, it may not toil in vain.

This is my theme, that such valor,
not shared among the others, is yours alone.
Thus declared Tullia on the Arno's banks.

VII

Ne vostro impero, anchor che bello, & raro,
Ne d'argento, & di gemme ampia ricchezza,
Che men da chi piu sa si brama, & prezza,
Vi fanno al mondo sì famoso & chiaro,

Quanto l'haver Signor pregiato, & caro,
La ben nata, & gentil anima avvezza
Con severa pietate, & dolce asprezza
Perdonar, & punir c'hoggi è si raro.

Queste vi fanno tal lunge, & d'appresso,
Ch'al grido sol del vostro nome altero
L'alma s'inchina, & come puo vi honora.

Et s'al caldo disio fia mai concesso
Stile al suggetto ugual, ritrarne spero
Fama immortal dopo la morte anchora.

VIII

Alla Illustrissima Signora Duchessa di Firenze

Non così d'acqua colmo in mar discende,
Ne di tante dorate arene vago
Si mostra al suo paese il ricco Tago,
Donde'l nome real di voi si prende,

Come del valor vostro a noi si stende
Di mille opre divine alto ampio lago:
Et quante (benche in dir nulla m'appago)
Bellezze scorge in voi chi dritto intende.

Quest'è l'arena d'oro, & queste l'onde
Di beltate & virtù, che'l bello & santo
Animo, & volto vostro a l'Arno infonde.

Non più la Spagna homai gioisca tanto,
Che s'ella ha'l Tago con l'aurate sponde,
LEONORA havrem noi con maggior vanto.

VII

Neither your empire, so fine and precious,
nor your ample riches of jewels and silver
that the least of those who know desire,
make you admired and illustrious.

It is your soul, Signor, so worthy and dear,
that the well-born one longs for so eagerly,
a soul tempered by sweet harshness and severe piety
and justice to pardon or punish, today so rare.

Because of these qualities, prized far and near,
at the proud sound of your name
my soul bows and honors you as it may.

And if it is granted, my heart's ardent desire
that my style should be worthy of my theme,
may immortal fame outlast death's sway.

VIII

To the Most Illustrious Signora Duchess of Florence[18]

The sea, full of water, does not descend
thus, nor do I desire the copious golden sands
that the rich Tagus's[19] realms can claim —
since from you they take their royal name.

Further does the ocean of your valor extend,
a high ample lake of a thousand works divine;
indescribable beauties in you they find
those who discern aright and understand.

This is the golden shore, and these the waves
infused into the Arno, by beauty and virtue graced,
and by your beautiful soul and holy face.

Nevermore will Spain have as much joy as is ours,
though she has the Tagus with its golden shores;
since we have LEONORA, the greater claim is ours.

IX

O qual vi debb'io dire o Donna o Diva?
Poi che tanta beltà, tanto valore[20]
Riluce in voi, che'l vostro almo splendore
Abbaglia qual fu mai fiamma piu viva?

Mi dice un bel pensier, che di voi scriva,
Et renda gratie, & qual si deve honore;
Ma dove s'erge l'animoso core,
Non giunge penna, o voce humana arriva.

So ch'ogni alto favor da voi mi viene,
Come la luce al dì da quella stella,
Che surge in Oriente innanzi al Sole.

Ma poi che pur al fin mal si conviene
A tanta altezza l'humil mia favella,
V'appaghi il core in vece di parole.

X

Donna reale, a i cui santi desiri
Gratia gia fece la bontà superna
Di me, c'hor fatta son chiara lucerna
Sopra i celesti, ardenti, alti zaphiri;

Poi che fuor di sospetto, & di martiri
Godo del ben, che ne l'alme s'interna,
Deh non turbate la mia pace eterna
Col pianto vostro, & co i vostri sospiri.

Quì mi viv'io, dove'l pensier non erra;
Dove luogo non ha terreno affetto;
Et co i piè calco gli stellanti chiostri.

Et se quà su giungesser gli occhi vostri,
Vedendo fatto me novo angeletto,
Quì bramareste, & non vedermi in terra.

IX

O Lady or Goddess, which is your name?
Since so much beauty and such valor are
reborn in you as light, your soul's splendor
is beyond all others, ever so bright a flame.

A beautiful thought tells me: *write,*
give thanks to her, the one whom I honor,
but neither pen nor tongue can render[21]
the thoughts that arise from a spirited heart.

From you, I know, comes all high favor,
like the light of the day from that star
that rises in the east before the sun.[22]

But since to this end it ill befits decorum
for my humble speech to rise to such a height,
instead of words, I pay the debt with my heart.

X

Noble lady, through whose high desires
heaven's bounty flows, its grace bestowing
on me, now made as a lamp, glowing
high above the heavens, burning sapphires;

Since beyond all suspicion and all sorrow
I rejoice in the good bowered in the soul,
do not disturb my state of peace eternal
with your sighs and plaints of life below.

Here I live, where thought does not err,
in a place by earthly desires unaffected,[23]
and with my feet trace cloisters made of stars.

And if your eyes reach the heavenly sphere,
on seeing me, an angel[24] newly perfected,
yearn to see me here, and not on Earth.

XI

S'a l'alto Creator de gli Elementi
Sete Donna Real contanto cara,
Che de la stirpe vostra altera, & rara
Volle ornare i suoi chiostri eterno ardenti.

Et s'hor per acquetar vostri lamenti,
Vi rende il cambio di quell'alma chiara,
Che di voi nata tutto'l Ciel rischiara,
A Dio lode cantando in dolci accenti.

Ragion è ben, che con eterni honori
Vi cantin tutti gli spirti piu rari,
Com'honorata in terra, e in ciel gradita.

Arno alzi l'acque al Ciel, le rive infiori;
Suonino i tempi, & fumino gli altari;
Che'l nuovo parto a festeggiar n'invita.

XII

Alla Illustrissima Signora Maria Salviati de' Medici

Anima bella, che dal padre eterno
Creata prima in Ciel nuda, e immortale,
Hor vestita di vel caduco, & frale
Mostri quà giuso il gran valore interno;

Da gli alti chiostri in questo basso inferno,
V si n'aggrava il rio peso mortale,
Scendesti a torne noia, e a darne l'ale
Al sommo bello, al sommo ben superno.

Chiunque te pur una volta mira
Sente sgombrar da l'alma ogni vil voglia,
Et arder tutta di celeste amore.

Dunque ver me col divin raggio spira
Del disiato tuo santo favore,
Ch'io voli al Ciel con la terrena spoglia.

XI

If the elemental great Creator
holds you, royal lady, so dear
that he adorns his shining eternal cloisters
with your offspring, so noble and rare,

and if to appease your lamentation
He renders in exchange a soul so luminous,
born to brighten all of creation,
to sing His praises in tones harmonious,

it stands to reason that in your honor
all the rarest spirits sing your praises:
how welcome in heaven, how honored on Earth.

The Arno lifts its waters, its banks in flower;
the temples resound, from the altars incense arises,
inviting all to celebrate this joyous new birth.[25]

XII

To the Most Illustrious Signora Maria Salviati de' Medici[26]

Beautiful soul, created in heaven
by our Father immortal and brought to birth,
now clothed with a veil, frail and ephemeral,
we need your inner valor here on Earth.

From heaven's choirs into this hell descend,
where one grows heavy in the soul;
give us wings to transcend these earthly ills
so to the highest beauty and the good we may ascend.

If one, even once, is shown your face,
her soul is unburdened of all ill will
and with celestial love is set aflame.

Therefore, inspire me with the divine ray
of your much longed-for favor, so I may
ascend to heaven in this mortal coil.

XIII *Al Signor Don Luigi di Toledo*

Spirto gentil, che dal natio terreno
La chiarezza del sangue, e dal Ciel chiara
Anima havesti, e a cui d'ogni piu rara
Virtù colmar le sante Muse il seno;

Poi che'l cor vostro è d'alto valor pieno,
Et real cortesia da voi s'impara,
Non mi sia prego vostra mente avara
Di cio, ch'altrui donando non vien meno.

Voi sete quel, c'havete ambe le chiavi
Di quegli eccelsi, & gloriosi Cori
Che fan piu ch'anchor mai felice l'Arno:

Hor volgetele a me così soavi,
Ch'entro raccolta mai non esca fuori:
Et prego humil non sia'l mio prego indarno.

XIV *Al Signor Don Pedro di Toledo*

Ben si richiede al vostro almo splendore
Del chiaro sangue, e a la virtù eccellente,
Che si canti Signore eternamente
Ne gioghi di Parnaso il vostro honore.

Ond'è ch'a dir di voi dentr'al mio core
S'accende ogn'hor un vivo foco ardente:
Ma come a l'alta impresa non si sente
L'anima ugual si spenge il novo ardore.

Non s'assicura nel profondo seno
Di vostre glorie entrar mia navicella
Sotto la scorta del mio cieco ingegno.

Solchi'l gran mar di vostre lodi a pieno
Piu felice alma, a cui piu chiara stella
Porga favore in piu securo legno.

XIII *To Signor Don Luigi of Toledo* [27]

Spirit, whose illustrious blood and celestial origin
bestow renown upon your native Spain,
O soul whose breast the holy Muses infuse
more than others with the soul's most rare virtues:

Since your heart brims over with valor,
and from you one learns royal courtesy,
I pray that your hungry mind will desire
the gift that enriches the giver infinitely.

As one who holds both keys [28]
of the highest and most glorious courts
that make the Arno rejoice again,

turn your favor to me so gently
that into the harvest's abundance I go forth:
And I humbly pray that my prayer is not in vain.

XIV *To Signor Don Pedro of Toledo* [29]

Well might one ask that the living splendor
of your soul, noble blood, and matchless
virtue be ever sung, Signor, so that your honor
resounds from both peaks of Parnassus, [30]

for to speak of you engenders in my heart
an ardent deathless flame.
But not feeling myself equal to the part,
new ardor becomes dampened, spent, and lame.

It is uncertain, doubts arise in the core of my heart,
that my little ship can enter such glorious seas
with my blind wit as its sole escort.

To plow the great waves of the sea of your praise
requires a more fortunate soul, a brighter star,
a more seaworthy vessel to carry it into port. [31]

XV   *A Monsignore Cardinal Bembo*

BEMBO, io che fino a quì da grave sonno
Oppressa vissi, anzi dormii la vita,
Hor da la luce vostra alma infinita,
O sol d'ogni saper maestro, & donno,

Desta apro gli occhi, si ch'aperti ponno
Scorger la strada di virtù smarrita:
Ond'io lasciato ove'l pensier m'invita
De la parte miglior per voi m'indonno;

Et quanto posso il piu mi sforzo anch'io,
Scaldarmi al lume di si chiaro foco
Per lasciar del mio nome eterno segno.

Et o non pur da voi si prenda a sdegno
Mio folle ardir, che se'l sapere è poco,
Non è poco Signor l'alto disio.

XVI   *Al Signor Ridolfo Baglioni*

Signore in cui valore, & cortesia
Giostrano insieme ogn'hor tanto ugualmente,
Che discerner non puote umana mente
Di qual di lor piu la vittoria sia;

Mia fredda Musa a voi già non s'invia
Per celebrar vostra virtute ardente;
Ma perch'in voi nomar conosce, & sente
Scorger nel vostro honor la gloria mia.

Ben porta nel mio core un caldo affetto
Il vivo lume vostro, ch'è si chiaro,
Che risplender si vede in ogni parte.

Ma prenda voi per degno alto suggetto
Chi al quieto Apollo è tanto caro,
Quanto voi sete al bellicoso Marte.

XV *To Monsignor Cardinal Bembo* [32]

Until now, BEMBO, oppressed by so deep a slumber,
I have lived, a sleepwalker through the caves
where thought resides; now may the infinite rays
of your soul shine forth through the penumbra,

and open my eyes so I can see straight ahead
to discern the road of virtue I'd mislaid, [33]
the road I'd left, where thought still invites me:
I am led to the better part, enticed by your nobility.

And how much more I, too, aspire
to warm myself in the light of such a flame —
to leave an eternal record of my name.

And yet, I have not met with your disdain;
though my knowledge is limited and my ardor vain,
there is no limit, Signor, to my high desire.

XVI *To Signor Ridolfo Baglioni* [34]

Signor, in whom valor and courtesy
joust together in such equal measure,
that no mortal mind can discern
which of them will win the victory.

My chilly Muse does not attend to you
to celebrate your burning virtue,
but the name all hear and know
is yours — from your honor, my glory flows.

Like a strong tonic warming my heart,
your vivid living light, so bright and clear,
is seen shining like the sun on every side.

So take this high theme as dignified,
from one who holds sober Apollo dear,
though you belong to warlike Mars. [35]

XVII *Al Signor Francesco Crasso*

La nobil valorosa antica gente,
Che di novo i fratelli ancisi vede,
Et in acerbo essilio a pianger riede,
Signore a te s'inchina humilemente.

Et potendo vendetta arditamente
Gridar de morti, & piaghe, & mille prede,
Mercè sola, & pietate a te richiede,
Di comune voler pietosamente.

O sanator de le ferite nostre
Mira la velenosa, e cruda rabbia,
Che'l sangue giusto ingiustamente sugge.

Così tosto avverrà, ch'in te si mostre,
Com'a gran torto tanti danni hor abbia
La gente, cui pietate & doglia strugge.

XVIII *Al Molza*

Poscia (ohime) che spento ha l'empia morte
L'alma gentil, ch'in sua piu verde etade
A gran passi salìa l'erte contrade,
Che menan dritto a la superna corte:

Chi fia che leggi così crude, & torte,
Spirti amici d'onor, & di bontade
Non pianga meco ogn'hor, ch'a le piu rade
Virtù die sempre il ciel vite piu corte?

MOLZA ben pianger dei poi ch'al camino,
Ove ti sprona un disusato ardire,
Perduta hai meco la piu fida scorta.

Io per me dopo si fero destino
Non voglio altro, non deggio che morire.
Se morir deve, & puote chi è già morta.

XVII *To Signor Francesco Crasso*[36]

The noble valorous ancient people,
who see their brothers killed anew
and in bitter exile return to weeping,
they bend their heads humbly, Signor, to you.

And if they could, they'd boldly cry *vendetta!*
for the thousand spoils, the wounded and the dead,
mercy of you alone is requested
by the people's common will, with *pietà.*

Observe, O healer of our wounds,
the cruel and poisonous rage,
and the blood of the just, unjustly sucked.[37]

Soon it will come to pass, as presaged,
the already-wronged will be dragged in muck—
those whom piety and sorrow now consume.

XVIII *To Molza*[38]

Alas, can it be that this noble soul,
spent by greedy death in his greenest years,
ascends with great steps the steep spheres
leading to heaven's courts celestial?

Kindred spirits of honor and generosity,
mourn with me, you who on virtue and honor thrive,
as I ask, *who makes these laws so cruel, whereby*
heaven gives the best spirits the shortest lives?

Well may you weep, MOLZA, for on the road,
spurred along with an unaccustomed goad,
you've lost, like me, your most trusted guide.

For my part, after such a fierce blow of destiny,
I wish for nothing, nothing remains for me
but to die—if one can or should, who is dead already.

XIX   *Al Signor Colonnello Luca Antonio*

Poi che rea sorte ingiustamente preme
Voi, ch'alto albergo sete di valore,
Sento spirto gentil un tal dolore,
Che con voi l'alma mia ne giace insieme.

L'anima mia ne giace, e'l petto geme
Di non poter mostrar nel viso il core
A voi, cui bramo con perpetuo honore
Piacer servendo infino a l'hore estreme.

Il disio d'hora in hora a voi mi porta:
Quindi rispetto honesto mi ritiene:
E di scuoter conviemmi quel ch'io voglio.

In si dubbioso stato mi conforta,
Che ben v'è noto quel che si conviene.
Et questo fa minore il mio cordoglio.

XX   *A Messer Ugolino Martelli*

Mentre ch'al suon de i dotti ornati versi
Fate d'Arno suonar l'ampie contrade,
Cantando insieme a piu ch'ad una etade
Con le virtu, ch'a voi si amiche fersi,

A me caro Martel son tanto adversi
I fati, ch'ogni ben dal cor mi cade;
E per occulte, solitarie strade
Vo lagrimando il dì, che gli occhi apersi.

Tal che del pianto mio, del mio languire
Languisce, & piagne ogni sterpo, & ogni sasso,
E le fiere, & gli augelli in ogni parte.

Voi, mentre afflige me l'empio martire,
Deh consolate lo mio spirto lasso
Con vostre eterne, & honorate carte.

XIX *To Signor Colonel Luca Antonio* [39]

Since you are by unjust fate oppressed,
you, whose breast is valor's seat,
I feel, noble soul, such a sorrowful weight
that my spirit lies with yours in the dust.

My spirit lies low, and inwardly I mourn,
unable to show you my heart in my face,
you, whom I desire to honor with grace
and serve until I am on Earth no more.

Desire brings me to you by degrees,
but honest respect holds the reins of my heart,
for that which I desire makes me tremble.

In such a dubious state I am able
to choose the more fitting part,
which lessens my sorrows and puts me at ease.

XX *To Messer Ugolino Martelli* [40]

The ample lands around the Arno reverberate
with the sound of your learned poems,
and the Virtues, singing for ages to come,
are your constant friends. But to me, the Fates

are so perverse that every good thing falls straight
from my hands, and along the solitary way
through hidden paths, I lament the day
that my eyes first opened and saw the light.

Such is my plaint that with every stone
and every broken twig grief weeps, [41]
and animals and birds in every glade moan.

As I am afflicted by pitiless wrongs,
console my soul, exhausted without sleep,
with your honored and everlasting songs.

XXI *Al Varchi*

VARCHI, da cui giamai non si scompagna
Il choro de le Muse, e ch'a l'affanno
Com'a la gioia, a l'util com'al danno,
Sempre havete virtù fida compagna:

Qual monte, o valle, o riviera, o campagna
Non sarà a voi piu che dorato scanno?
Se come fumo innanzi a lei sen vanno
Gli humani affetti, ond'altri più si lagna.

O perche errar a me così non lice
Con voi pe i boschi, come ho'l core acceso
De l'honorate vostre fide scorte?

C'havendo ogni pensiero al cielo inteso
Vivendo viverei vita felice,
Et morta sperarei vincer la morte.

XXII

VARCHI il cui raro, & immortal valore
Ogni anima gentil subito invoglia,
Deh perche non poss'io com'ho la voglia
Del vostro alto saver colmarmi il core?

Che con tal guida so ch'uscirei fore
De le man di fortuna che mi spoglia
D'ogni usato conforto: e ogni mia doglia
Cangerei in dolce canto, e'n miglior hore.

Ahi lassa, io veggio ben che la mia sorte
Contrasta a così honesto; & bel desire,
Sol perche manch'io sotto l'aspre some.

Ma s'a me pur così convien finire
La penna vostra al men levi il mio nome
Fuor de gli artigli d'importuna morte.

XXI *To Varchi*[42]

VARCHI, never alone, always the Muses' minion;
in labor as in joy, when you are well
no less than when beset by ills,
with Virtue as your faithful companion:

What mountain or valley, countryside or river
would not be your gilded Arcadian[43] throne?
If human affections dissipate, ephemeral as vapor,
why more than others do you lament and moan?[44]

Because I cannot be your faithful guide
through the woods, my spirits light,
and wander freely by your side?

If all my prayers were by heaven heard,
then living, I'd live happy with every breath,
and dying, I would hope to conquer death.

XXII

VARCHI, whose valor immortal and rare
quickly enfolds every noble soul,
why am I unable to fulfill my desire
and with your wisdom my heart fill?

For with such a guide, I would be free
from Fortune's talons, sharp and long,
despoiling me hourly of everything sweet,
and my sorrow would change key, into a lighter song.

Alas, I see clearly that unjust fate assails me,
contrary to my every honest high desire,
and under such harsh burdens my strength fails me.

But if it is fitting, even with my final breath
I ask that you lift up my name with your pen,
safe from the claws of untimely death.[45]

XXIII

Dopo importuna pioggia
S'allegrano i pastor, quando'l sereno
    Ciel si discopre lor di stelle pieno.
Et dopo'l corso de l'instabil luna
    Ne l'apparir del Sole
    Gioisce ogni animal che brama il giorno,
Et l'alto Dio lodar ben spesso suole
    Dopo l'aspra fortuna
    Spaventato nocchier al porto intorno.
E'l VARCHI è al suo ritorno
    Seren, sol, porto; & chi ha d'honor disio;
Si rallegra, gioisce, e loda Dio.

XXIV   *Al Muzio*

Voi, ch'havete fortuna si nimica,
Com'animo valor e cortesia,
Qual benigno destino hoggi m'invia
A riveder la vostra fiamma antica?

MUTIO gentile, una alma, così amica
E soave valore a l'alma mia.
Ben duolmi de la dura, e alpestra via
Con tanta non di voi degna fatica.

Visse gran tempo l'honorato amore
Ch'al Po gia per me v'arse. Et non cred'io
Che sia si chiara fiamma in tutto spenta.

Et se nel volto altrui si legge il core,
Spero ch'in riva d'Arno il nome mio
Alto sonar anchor per voi si senta.

XXIII

After unexpected rain
the shepherds rejoice, when serene
    heaven uncovers itself, revealing a star-filled sky.
And after the course of the mutable moon,
    in the shining forth of the sun,
      every creature rejoices that longs for the day.
And praising God most high,
    as after bitter misfortune,
      the frightened helmsman to his port returns.
And, at VARCHI's return,
    serene, the port and sun; and the one
who looks for honor rejoices, exults, and praises God.

XXIV   *To Muzio*[46]

You who are held in enmity, fortune's foe,
but full of courtesy and valor all the same,
what uncommon stroke of good luck moves you
to kindle once more your ancient flame?[47]

Noble MUZIO, spirit so kindred and true,
so gentle a balm to my own soul,
how I lament the harshness of the road,
and that toil so unworthy of you.

It was a long-lived and honored love
that burned for me by the Po.[48] No,
I do not believe that its flame is quite spent.

If from your face one can read your intent,
I hope to hear my name sung with love
from your lips on the banks of the Arno.

XXV *Al Predicator Ochino*

BERNARDO, ben potea bastarvi haverne
Co'l dolce dir, ch'a voi natura infonde,
Quì dove'l Re de' fiumi ha piu chiare onde,
Acceso i cuori a le sante opre eterne.

Che se pur sono in voi pur l'interne
Voglie, e la vita al vestir corrisponde,
Non huom di frale carne, & d'ossa immonde,
Ma sete un voi de le schiere superne.

Hor le finte apparenze, e'l ballo, e'l suono
Chiesti dal tempo, & da l'antica usanza
A che così da voi vietati sono?

Non fora santità, fora arroganza
Torre il libero arbitrio, il maggior dono,
Che Dio ne diè ne la primiera stanza.

XXVI *A Messer Emilio Tondi*

Siena dolente i sui migliori invita
A lagrimar intorno al su gran TONDI,
Al cui valor ben furo i Ciel secondi,
Poscia invidiaro l'honorata vita.

Marte il pianger di lei co'l pianto aita
Morto'l campion, cui fur gli altri secondi;
Io prego i miei sospir caldi, & profondi,
Ch'a sfogar si gran duol porgano aita.

So che non pon recar miei tristi accenti
A voi Messer EMILIO alcun conforto,
Che fra tanti dolori il primo è'l vostro.

Ma'l duol si tempri; il suo mortale è morto;
Vive'l suo nome eterno fra le genti;
L'alma triompha nel superno chiostro.

XXV   *To the preacher Ochino* [49]

BERNARDO, it should have been enough for you —
with your sweet speech, by nature infused,
here by the famous waters of the king of rivers —
to set hearts aflame to deeds holy and true.

And yet, if your desires are pure within
if your inner life matches your outer robes,
you are not a man of worldly flesh and bone
but from the highest ranks of seraphim.

Costumes, masquerades, and music sweetly played,
sanctioned by use and by custom honored still —
why do you prohibit these ancient pastimes?

It is not holiness, but arrogance displayed
to take away the greatest gift — free will —
bestowed by God from the beginning of time.

XXVI   *To Messer Emilio Tondi* [50]

Siena, lamenting, summons its best men
to mourn great TONDI with sorrowful lament,
to whose record of valor the heavens come second,
and such honor made manifest is worthy of envy.

Mourning his champion, Mars joins the throng,
weeping with Siena as the others follow;
I pray that my sighs, profound and low,
express the collective grief in song.

My sad accents do not comfort or reassure,
Messer EMILIO, nor do they bring relief,
For among these sorrows, the greatest is yours.

May your sorrow be tempered and mortal, death's grief,
may his name live on in memory, eternal,
and may his soul triumph in its cloister supernal.

XXVII *A Tiberio Nari*

Se veston sol d'eterna gloria il manto
Quei, che l'honor più che la vita amaro,
Perche volete voi gentil mio NARO
Render men bella con acerbo pianto

Quella lode immortale, & chiara tanto,
Di cui mai non sarà chi giunga al paro
Del valoroso vostro fratel caro,
Che morendo portò di morte'l vanto?

Scacciate'l duol; rasserenate il volto;
Et le unite da lui nemiche spoglie
Sacrate a lui, che gia trionfa in Cielo.

Et da questa mortal caduco velo
Piu che mai vivo, o mai libero, & sciolto
Par ch'a seguirlo ogni bell'alma invoglie.

XXVIII *A Piero Manelli*

Poi che mi diè natura a voi simile
Forma, & materia; o fosse il gran Fattore;
Non pensate ch'anchor disio d'honore
Mi desse, & bei pensier MANEL gentile?

Dunque credete me cotanto vile,
Ch'io non osi mostrar cantando fore,
Quel che dentro n'ancide altero ardore,
Se bene a voi non ho pari lo stile?

Non lo crediate, no, PIERO, ch'anch'io
Fatico ognihor per appressarmi al Cielo,
E lasciar del mio nome in terra fama.

Non contenda rea sorte il bel desio,
Che pria che l'alma dal corporeo velo
Si scioglia, satierò forse mia brama.

XXVII *To Tiberio Nari* [51]

Only those who love honor more than life
are clothed with eternal glory's mantle.
So why do you wish me to sing, most gentle
NARI, and render less lovely with bitter grief

such praise, immortal and most
famous, in honor of one without peer,
your brother, valorous and dear,
who dying, made death his boast?

Banish sorrow, make your face serene again,
for gathered by him are the enemy spoils;
consecrated to him who triumphs in heaven

more alive than ever, free from the bodily veil
and induced to follow all beautiful souls
no longer enveloped in this mortal coil.

XXVIII *To Piero Manelli* [52]

Since, like you, by Nature I was wrought —
or by the Great Creator — in Form and Matter,
MANELLI dear, do you think the desire for honor
was not also given me — and capacity for lofty thought?

Do you think me so spiritually poor
that I dare not show forth, singing,
what in me would extinguish all proud longing
though my style is not on par with yours?

No, I do not think you can conceive, PIERO,
that I, too, labor — aspire to reach the firmament,
and to leave my name renowned on Earth.

If evil fate does not triumph over high desire,
then perhaps before my soul is rent
from its corporeal veil, I will satisfy this thirst. [53]

XXIX

Amore un tempo in così lento foco
Arse mia vita; & sì colmo di doglia
Struggeasi'l cor, che quale altro si voglia
Martir fora ver lei dolcezza, & gioco.

Poscia sdegno, & pietate a poco a poco
Spenser la fiamma, ond'io più ch'altra soglia
Libera da sì lunga, & fera voglia
Giva lieta cantando in ciascun loco.

Ma'l Ciel ne satio anchor (lassa) ne stanco
De danni miei, perche sempre sospiri
Mi riconduce a la mia antica sorte.

E con sì acuto spron mi punge il fianco,
Ch'io temo sotto i primi empii martiri
Cader, & per men mal bramar la morte.

XXX

Qual vaga Philomena, che fuggita
È da l'odiata gabbia, & in superba
Vista se n'va tra gli arboscelli, & l'herba
Tornata in libertate, e in lieta vita;

Er'io da gli amorosi lacci uscita
Schernendo ogni martire, & pena acerba
De l'incredibil duol, ch'in se riserba
Qual ha per troppo amar l'alma smarrita.

Ben havev'io ritolte (ahi Stella fera)
Dal tempio di Ciprigna le mie spoglie,
E di lor pregio me n'andava altera;

Quand'a me Amor, *le tue retrose voglie,*
Muterò disse, & femmi prigionera
Di tua virtù, per rinovar mie doglie.

XXIX

Love, for a time, with its slow fierce flame
burned my life, and my heart, laden so,
fed on itself, so that all other sorrow
seemed but sweetness and a game.

Then, by degrees, piety and disdain
spent that flame — and freed from the fire
of such a great and fierce desire,
I went everywhere, singing with joy again.

But heaven, not weary (alas) nor satisfied
with my torments and continual sighs
brought me back once more to my ancient fate,

and with such a sharp spur pierced my side[54]
that I feared I'd fall from the blow's first spate.
And from lesser ills, I would hope to die.

XXX

Like flitting Philomel,[55] who goes so proudly free,
having escaped the prison of her hated cage,
who flies above the wooded grove and stone cottage,
returning to her former happy life in liberty —

so had I escaped from love's handcuffs,
scorning all suffering and the bitter pain,
the sorrow beyond belief reserved for one
who has lost her soul through excess, loving love.

As the Cyprian[56] knows well (oh, merciless star!)
I had gathered up my spoils from her temple
and for their price I had gone proud and far

when to me Love said: *I will alter*
(to renew my pangs) *your perverse will,*
and made me your virtue's prisoner.

XXXI

Felice speme, ch'a tant'alta impresa
Ergi la mente mia, ch'adhor adhora
Dietro al santo pensier, che la innamora,
Sen'vola al Ciel per contemplare intesa.

De bei disir in gentil foco accesa
Miro ivi lui, ch'ogni bell'alma honora.
Et quel ch'è dentro, & quanto appar di fora
Versa in me gioia senz'alcuna offesa.

Dolce, che mi feristi, aurato strale,
Dolce, ch'inacerbir mai non potranno
Quante amarezze dar puote aspra sorte.

Pro mi fia grande ogni piu grave danno;
Che del mio ardir per haver merto eguale
Piu degno guiderdon non è che morte.

XXXII

S'io'l feci unqua, che mai non giunga a riva
L'interno duol, che'l cuor lasso sostiene:
S'io'l feci, che perduta ogni mia spene
In guerra eterna de vostr'occhi viva;

S'io'l feci; ch'ogni dì resti piu priva
De la gratia, onde nasce ogni mio bene;
S'io'l feci, che di tante, & cotai pene
Non m'apporti alcun mai tranquilla oliva;

S'io'l feci, ch'in voi manchi ogni pietade;
Et cresca doglia in me, pianto, e martire
Distruggendomi pur come far soglio.

Ma s'io no'l feci, il duro vostro orgoglio
In amor si converta; & lunga etade
Sia dolce il frutto del mio bel disire.

XXXI

Felicitous Hope, which lifts my mind
to such high tasks that hour by hour
by holy thoughts enamored
she soars skyward in contemplation divine.

O high desire, lit by a noble flame,
I admire the One whom every lovely soul honors
And that which is within, as much as is apparent,
turn to joy in me, without offense.

Sweet, who wounds me, golden arrow,[57]
sweet, despite fate's harsh and bitter blows,
I could never be embittered towards you.

Let fall upon me every harm, great and grave,
hoping for merit equal to ardor, I give my faith,
no token of which is worthier than death.

XXXII

If I ever did it, then the sorrow will never end,
and my weary heart sustains its inner strife;
if I did it, then all my hope is lost, and
I live in perpetual warfare with your eyes.

If I did it, then every day I remain
more deprived of grace-bearing good;
if I did it, so much sorrow, such pain
will never bring the tranquil olive branch.

If I did it, then in you all piety is denied
and sorrow grows in me, tears and suffering
consuming me as if they never tire.

But if I didn't do it, then your harsh pride
will change to love, a season long in ripening;
so may it be sweet, the fruit of my high desire.[58]

XXXIII

Se ben pietosa madre unico figlio
Perde talhora, e nuovo alto dolore
Le preme il tristo & suspiroso core
Spera conforto almen, spera consiglio;

Se scaltro Capitano in gran periglio
Mostrando alteramente il suo valore
Resta vinto, & prigion, spera uscir fuore
Quando che sia con baldanzoso ciglio:

S'in tempestoso mar giunto si duole
Spaventato Nocchier gia presso a morte,
Ha speme anchor di rivedersi in porto.

Ma io, s'avvien che perda il mio bel Sole,
O per mia colpa, o per malvagia sorte,
Non spero haver, ne voglio alcun conforto.

XXXIV

Se forse per pietà del mio languire
Al suon del tristo pianto in questo loco
Ten'vieni a me, che tutta fiamma, e foco
Ardomi, e struggo colma di disire,

Vago augellino, & meco il mio martire
Ch'in pena volge ogni passato gioco,
Piangi cantando in suon dolente, & roco,
Veggendomi del duol quasi perire;

Pregoti per l'ardor, che si m'addoglia
Ne voli in quella amena, & cruda valle,
Ov'è chi sol puo darmi, & morte, & vita;

Et cantando gli dì, che cangi voglia
Volgendo a Roma'l viso, e a lei le spalle,
Se vuol l'alma, trovar col corpo unita.

XXXIII

If a loving mother, her only child lost,
feels anew the press of grief's weight
against her sad and sighing heart,
she hopes for comfort—for counsel, at least.

If a cunning captain finds himself in danger,
having shown in proud battle his valor in vain,
even if vanquished, languishing in prison,
he hopes with brave brow his escape is arranged.

If a sailor[59] braves the tempestuous ocean,
afraid that death is near and land is far,
still he hopes to see himself safe in port.

But if I should ever lose my lovely Sun[60]
by my own fault or by fate's treacherous star,
I do not hope for, nor desire, comfort.

XXXIV

If perhaps you feel pity for my weakness
at the sound of my plaint, here in this place,
come to me, all fire and flame,
I burn and am yet whole, by desire consumed.

Free-hearted bird, these trials have changed
all my heart's past lightness into present pain;
hoarse with the sounds of sorrowful singing;
seeing me almost perish from grief, weep with me.

Half-dead from the strain, I pray you, come fly
to me in this pleasant rustic valley, come,
you, who make me live or die at will.

I sing the days that you might change your will.
Turn your shoulders to her and your face to Rome,
if you wish to reunite your body with her soul.[61]

XXXV

Ov'è (misera me) quell'aureo crine,
Di cui fe rete per pigliarmi Amore?
Ov'è (lassa) il bel viso, onde l'ardore
Nasce, che mena la mia vita al fine?

Ov'è son quelle luci alte, e divine,
In cui dolce si vive, e insieme more?
Ov'è la bianca man, che lo mio core
Stringendo punse con acute spine?

Ov'è suonan l'angeliche parole
Ch'in un momento mi dan morte, & vita?
V i cari sguardi? u le maniere belle?

Ov'è luce hora il vivo almo mio Sole,
Con cui dolce destin mi venne in sorte
Quanto mai piovve da benigne stelle?

XXXVI

Se materna pietate afflige il core,
Onde cercando in questa parte, e in quella
Il caro figlio tuo LILLA mia bella
Piangi, & cresci piangendo il tuo dolore;

A te, ch'animal sei di ragion fore,
Et non intendi (ohime) quanto rubella
Sia stata ad ambe noi sorte empia, & fella,
Togliendo a te'l tuo figlio, a me'l mio Amore;

Che far (lassa) degg'io? qual degno pianto
Verseran gli occhi miei dal cor mai sempre?
Che conosco il tuo male, e'l mio gran danno.

Chi di Psichi potrà con alto canto
Cantar l'altere lodi? o con quai tempre
Temprar quel, che mi da sua morte, affanno?

XXXV

Where is that mane of golden curls
of which love made a net to entrap me?[62]
Where is, alas, that lovely face, in which was born
the very ardor that brought my life to its close?

Where are those lights, so splendid and divine,
in which one sweetly lives and in them dies?
Where, the sweet hand, this heart embracing,
yet punctured it with the sharpest thorns?

Where, the sound of the angelic words
that in a moment give me death and life?
Where, the sweet glances and the charming ways?

Where now the light, the living soul, my Sun?
With what sweet destiny comes my fate to me,
how much will it rain from such fortunate stars?

XXXVI

If maternal sorrow afflicts your heart,
as you look, seeking
your dear son, my lovely LILLA,[63]
you grieve, and your grief grows, weeping.

If you, an animal devoid of reason,
do not understand (alas) how it can be
that we are dealt one hand by fate's treason,
taking from you your son, my love from me,[64]

then what should I do, what worthy elegy
streams forth from my heart through my eyes?
For I know your pain, and my great injury.

And who will sing of Psyche, a song beyond death
in proud praise of her labors?[65] In what timbre or key
temper that which kills me, makes me labor for breath?

XXXVII

Alma del vero bel chiara sembianza,
A cui non puo far scherno nè riparo
Così gentile, & christallina stanza,
Che non mostri di fuor l'altero, & raro
Splendor, che sol ne da ferma speranza
Del ben, ch'unqua non fura il tempo avaro;
Deh fa se morta m'hai, ch'in te rinuovi
Accio di doppia morte il viver pruovi.

XXXVIII

Ben mi credea fuggendo il mio bel Sole
scemar (misera me) l'ardente foco
Con cercar chiari rivi, & starne a l'ombra
Ne i più fronzuti, & solitarii Boschi;
Ma quanto più lontan lace il suo raggio
Tanto più, d'hor in hor cresce'l mio vampo.

Chi crederebbe mai che questo vampo
Crescesse quanto è piu lontan dal Sole?
E pur il provo, che quel divin raggio
Quant'è piu lunge piu raddoppia il foco.
Ne mi giova habitar fontane, o boschi,
Ch'al mio mal nulla val, fresco, onda, od ombra.

Ma non cercherò piu fresco, onda, od ombra,
Che'l mio così cocente, & fero vampo
Non ponno ammorzar punto fonti, o boschi:
Ma ben seguirò sempre il mio bel Sole,
Poscia che nuova Salamandra in foco
Vivo lieta, mercè del divo raggio.

XXXVII

Soul, a radiant semblance of the truth,
whom none can guard against or screen;
so noble, so crystalline-pure a room
that your splendor does not show forth[66]
and alone gives steadfast hope of the good;
you, so rare, so proud and pure,
safe from greedy time which devours —
if you have my death, then may something of it be renewed
in you of that second death[67] the living undergo.

XXXVIII

I thought, fleeing my beloved Sun,
to diminish (O misery!) this constant fire
by seeking clear rivers and staying in the shadows
in the most leafy, the most lonely woods;
but the further away extend his shining rays
the stronger, hour by hour, grows my flame.

Who would believe that this flame
increases with distance from the sun?
And yet the further extends this divine ray,
the more it redoubles its fire.
It does me no good to haunt fountain or wood;
worthless in my pain are breezes, waves, and shade.

I no longer seek fresh breezes, waves, or shade,
for my blazing and fierce flame
cannot be quenched in stream or wood;
always will I follow my beloved Sun,
for as a salamander lives anew in fire,[68]
I live in joy, thanks to his divine ray.

Deh perche non m'alluma il vivo raggio
Ovunqu'io vado, o per sole, o per ombra?
Che lieta soffrirei sì dolce il foco,
Et contenta morrei del suo gran vampo.
Ma non spero giamai (lassa) che'l Sole
Scopra giorno sì chiaro in questi boschi.

Ond'havrò sempre in odio i monti, e i boschi
Che m'ascondon la luce di quel raggio,
Che splende, & scalda piu de l'altro Sole.
Biasmi chi vuole, & fugga i raggi a l'ombra,
Ch'io per me cerco sempre, & lodo il vampo,
Che m'arde, & strugge in sì possente foco.

Quanto dunque mi fora grato il foco,
Ingrati i monti, & le fontane, e i boschi,
V non veggo il mio Sole, & sento il vampo.
S'io potessi appressar l'amato raggio,
Et del mio stesso corpo a lui far ombra,
Et quando parte, & quando torna il Sole.

Prima fia oscuro il Sole, & freddo il foco,
Ne faranno ombra in nessun tempo i boschi,
Che del bel raggio in me non arda il vampo.

Then why does it not illuminate me, the living ray,
wherever I go, in sunlight or in shadow?
With pleasure would I suffer such a sweet fire [69]
and die content from its great flame.
But I do not hope (alas) to see the sun
unveil so bright a day in these woods.

I will hold in hatred the mountains and the woods
that hide from me the light of this bright ray,
which shines and burns more than the other sun.
Blame me if you wish, flee these rays for shade,
but as for me, I'll always seek and praise the flame
that burns me, and be consumed in such a potent fire.

Therefore, so gracious to me is this fire
that unkind are the mountains, streams, and woods
where I cannot see my Sun, but feel his flame.
If only I could come nearer to the beloved ray
and of my own body make for him a shade
both at the setting and the rising of the sun.

But the sun would become dark, and cold, the fire,
and never would there be a shadow in the woods
before this lovely ray no longer burns in me, this flame.

... Et di Diversi a Lei

Sonnets by Diverse Poets to Tullia with Her Responses

Lattanzio de Benucci a Tullia

Deh non volgete altrove il dotto stile
Altera donna, ch'a voi stessa, poi
Che scorge il mondo esser accolto in voi
Quant'ha del pellegrino & del gentile.

Appo questo suggetto incolto, & vile
Divien qual piu pregiato hoggi è tra noi:
Et co'l splendor de' vivi raggi suoi
Chiaro si mostra ognihor da Battro a Thile.

Voi dunque di voi sola alzare il nome
Dovete, poi ch'a sì pregiato segno
Giunger non puote il piu purgato inchiostro.

Quindi vedrassi apertamente come
Non è di lode altri di voi piu degno;
Ne stil, che giunga al dolce cantar vostro.

Tullia a Lattantio Bennucci

Io, ch'a ragion tengo me stessa a vile,
Ne scorgo parte in me, che non m'annoi
Bramando torni[72] a morte, & viver poi
Ne le carte d'un qualche a voi simile,

Cercando vo per questo lieto Aprile
D'ingegni mille, non pur uno a doi
Suggetti degni dei piu alti Heroi,
E d'inchiostro al mio tutto dissimile.

Però dovunque avien, che mai si nome
Alteramente alcuno, indi m'ingegno
Trar rime, onde s'eterni il nome nostro.

Et spero ancor, se'l mio cangiar di chiome
Non rende pigro questo ardito ingegno,
D'Helicona salire al sacro chiostro.

Lattanzio de Benucci[70] to Tullia

Proud lady, do not turn your gifted style
to any use but your own; give not pearls to swine,
since the world discerns that with equity sublime
you welcome the pilgrim soul and the noble one.

I set forth my subject, so low in style,
yet more prized among us day by day;
may the splendor of your living ray
shine forth, in fame from Kabul to Thule.[71]

And thus your own name should you raise:
a worthy sign, a goal so prized,
that the highest choirs cannot come close.

Thus, as we will see quite openly, the praise
of others is not your talent's most worthy use.
What style can match your own sweet voice?

Tullia to Lattanzio Bennucci

With such good reason to hold myself as base,
I find no part of myself that does not give
me grief; desiring death, I long to live
through my poems alone or among your pages.

All this lovely April I go wandering and seek
ideas, yet not one among a thousand do I find;
it seems high subjects worthy of chivalric rhyme
come from heroic pens, dissimilar to mine in ink.

But come what may, never shall I wear my fame
so proudly that my talent does not bring forth
poems, whereby I may immortalize your name.

Though my hair turn white, let not this mind that soars
grow dull, nor burn with less intent a flame,
lest it prevent my ascent to Helicon's[73] sacred choirs.

Muzio a Tullia

Donna, il cui gratioso, e altero aspetto
E'l parlar pien d'angelica harmonia
Scorgon qual alma presso a lor s'invia
A contemplare il ben de l'intelletto,

Deh così amor non mai v'ingombri'l petto
D'humil disir, ne mai di gelosia
Gustiate'l tosco: & sempre intenta sia
A l'interna beltade il vostro affetto;

Date vi prego a me vera novella
De l'alma mia, che del mio core uscita
Voi seguendo è venuta a farsi bella.

Che se da voi la misera è sbandita,
Ella senza voi stando, & io senz'ella
Non ritrovo al mio scampo alcuna aita.

Tullia a Muzio

Spirto gentil, che vero, & raro oggetto
Sei di quel bel, che piu l'alma disia,
Et di cui brama ognihor la mente mia
Essere al tuo cantar caro suggetto;

Se di pari n'andasse in me l'effetto
Con le tue lode, honor render potria
Mia penna a te: ma poi mia sorte ria
M'ha si bramato honor tutto interdetto,

Sol dirò, che seguendo la sua stella
L'anima tua da te fece partita
Venendo in me com'in su propria, ella.

Et la mia, c'hora è teco insieme unita,
Ten'puo far chiara fede, come quella,
Che con la tua si mosse a cangiar vita.

Muzio[74] to Tullia

Lady, whose gracious and proud aspect
and speech, full of angelic harmony,
discerns that soul nearby that ascends
to contemplation of the good of intellect:

So may your heart, my love, never be heavy
with unworthy desire, may you never taste
the poison of jealousy, may your chaste
affection be ever intent on inner beauty.

Give me, I pray you, true news of my soul,
which, having gone out from my heart
and following you, has become beautiful.

Your soul, free from misery, is yet alive,
but if mine is apart from you, and I from her,
then nothing avails me, though I survive.

Tullia to Muzio

Noble soul for whom my spirit longs,
the object of my innermost desires,
of beauty so rare and true: my mind aspires
to be the theme of your sweetest songs.

If, wrought in me, is the same effect,
then I can render your praises with my pen,
though my cursèd fate prevents
our longed-for honor and respect.

I only ask that your soul, following her star
with steadfast faith, that your soul leave you
and come into my soul as if it were hers.

And mine, now united with yours,
holds fast the bright faith my soul gives ours:
joining souls, my life changes with yours.

Alessandro Arrighi a Tullia

S'un medesimo stral duo petti aprio,
S'arse duo cor d'amor un foco santo;
Se nascendo'l piacer mori cotanto
Martir, che l'uno & l'altro gia sentio:

Donna & s'in somma nudrì ambo un disio,
Ond'è ch'in me del dir vostro altrettanto
Non rivolgete si, ch'io mi dia vanto
D'esser d'huom fatto un immortale Dio?

Forse si come sempre hebbi nimica
La stella a i miei disir, così aven hora
Ch'io non goda, & non sorti una tal brama.

O pur ch'ad alma si saggia, & pudica
Parlar di me basso suggetto fora;
Come che sia il bel vostro a se mi chiama.

Tullia a Alessandro Arrighi

Spirto gentil, s'al giusto voler mio
Non è cortese il cielo, e amico tanto,
Ch'io possa con ragion lodarvi quanto
Me fate, & io far voi spero, & disio,

Dolgomi del mio fato acerbo, & rio,
Che cio mi niega rivolgendo in pianto
Il mio gia lieto, & dilettoso canto,
Per cui fan gli occhi miei si largo rio.

Ma se fortuna mai si mostra amica
A le mie voglie, non dubito ancora
Poter cantarvi tal qual mio cor brama,

E far sentir per questa piaggia aprica
Quant'è'l valor, ch'in voi mio core honora,
Piacciavi s'hor lo riverisce, & ama.

Alessandro Arrighi[75] to Tullia

If with the same arrow two breasts are pierced,
if two hearts burn with the same holy fire,
if pleasure, being born, is doomed to die
in the same pain that both experience;

Lady, if two hearts nourish one desire,
what avails me if you say otherwise?
Do not change so, lest I elevate my boast
from that of a man to a god metamorphosed.

If the stars remain ever cruel and hostile,
to my desires, as in the past and now,
without joy, I languish, fruitless and sterile.

Speaking of myself to a soul so true,
so modest and yet wise, I feel so base and low;
how is it your beauty yet calls me to you?

Tullia to Alessandro Arrighi

Noble soul, if heaven does not grant my most
just request, it is friendly enough to allow
me to praise you as best as I know how,
since you inspire me, and I make you, desire and hope,

My bitter and evil fate causes me to sorrow,
and this negates me, turning my song to lament
which, once delightful and content,
now from my eyes makes a great river flow.

But if fortune ever waxes amicable
to me, I do not yet doubt that I will be able
to sing to my heart's content

and make resound, throughout this vacant
lonely strand, how my heart cherishes your valor
and is pleased to pay respects of love and honor.

Niccolò Martelli a Tullia

Se'l mondo diede alhor la gloria a ARPINO
D'eloquenza immortale alta, & profonda,
La vostra al nome egual gli vien seconda
TULLIA di sangue illustre & pellegrino;

Il cui spirto reale almo & divino
Sovra l'uso mortal di gratie abonda,
In guisa tal, che l'honorata sponda
De l'Arbia infino al ciel tocca il confino.

E'l bel chiaro Arno, hora di voi s'honora,
L'antico fuor trahendo humido crine
Forma con l'acque in suon cotai parole;

Qual luce è questa o beltà senza fine,
Che col sommo valor le rive infiora
Al gel, come d'April nel mezo il Sole?

Tullia a Niccolò Martelli

Ben fu felice vostro alto destino,
Poi che vena vie die tanto feconda,
Che'l santo Apollo il vostro dir seconda
Piu ch'ei non fece al suo diletto Lino.

Il choro de le muse a capo chino
Lieto v'honora, e'l bel crin vi circonda
Di vaghi fiori, & d'odorata fronda:
Perche ragion è ben s'a voi m'inchino.

Il cantar vostro l'anime innamora;
E le fa da se stesse pellegrine
Che celeste virtù puo, cio che vuole.

E'n voi mirando gratie si divine
Chi ha piu gentil spirto piu v'honora.
Altri d'invidia si lamenta & dole.

Niccolò Martelli[76] to Tullia

If the world attributes glory to ARPINIUM[77]
of eloquence high, immortal, and profound,
then those of the same name come second
to TULLIA of noble blood, a royal pilgrim

whose regal spirit and divine *anima*[78]
abound with grace beyond mortal use, even
in human guise, as the shores of the Arbia
extend to touch the confines of heaven,

and the lovely clear Arno, which you now honor,
drawing forth antiquity in its laurelled Academy,[79]
forms with its waters words so exquisite.

What light is this, what beauty infinite,
what consummate valor makes the riverbanks flower
even in frost, as bright as the April sun at midday?

Tullia to Niccolò Martelli

So has fortune favored your high destiny,
and your veins given such fecundity
that holy Apollo follows your rhymes
more than he delights in Linus's[80] poems.

The chorus of the Muses bows its head happily
and honors your lovely locks, in garlands
of delightful flowers and pungent leafy fronds,
and so with reason, I bow down willingly.

Your singing so enamors other souls
that they become pilgrims through the celestial .
virtue heaven inspires, when it wills.

Seeing your graces are so divinely sent,
that the noblest spirits are most most moved to honor,
while others, out of envy, can only lament.

Lasca a Tullia

Se'l vostro alto valor Donna gentile
Esser lodato pur dovesse in parte,
Vopo sarebbe al fin vergar le carte
Col vostro altero[81] & glorioso stile.

Dunque voi sola a voi stessa simile,
A cui s'inchina la natura, & l'arte
Fate di voi cantando in ogni parte
TULLIA, suonar da Gange a Thile.

Si vedrem poi di gioia & maraviglia,
Et di gloria, & di honore il mondo pieno
Drizzare al vostro nome altare, & tempi.

Cosa che mai con l'ardenti sue ciglia
Non vide il Sol rotando il Ciel sereno,
O ne gli antichi, o ne moderni tempi.

Tullia a Lasca

Io, che fin quì quasi alga ingrata, & vile
Sprezzava in me così l'interna parte,
Come u di fuor, che tosto invecchia, & parte
Da noi ben spesso nel piu bello Aprile,

Hoggi LASCA gentil non pur a vile
Non mi tengo (mercè de le tue carte)
Ma movo ancor la penna ad honorarte,
Fatta in tutto a me stessa dissimile.

Et come, pianta, che suggendo piglia
Novo licor da l'humido terreno,
Manda fuor frutti, & fior, benche s'attempi.

Tal 'io potrei, si nuovo mi bisbiglia
Pensier nel cor di non venir mai meno,
Dar forse ancor di me non bassi esempi.

Lasca[82] to Tullia

If your high valor, Lady so noble,
is to be praised in part or in full,
it would take all the pages ever ruled
to honor your proud and glorious style.

Your only model is yourself, to whose rule
nature and art in courtesy bow down;
so sung everywhere, your name resounds,
TULLIA from the Ganges to the isle of Thule.[83]

We will see with wonder the glory of your fame,
and with joy and honor in ages to come:
altars and temples built in your name.

Such a thing, orbiting the heavens serene,
either in ancient or modern times,
the Sun's ardent brow has never seen.

Tullia to Lasca

Until now, I held my soul as vile, ungrateful,
despising and scorning the inner part
as much as the outer, as we grew old and apart
from each other in that most beautiful April.

Today, noble LASCA, I do not hold myself
of so little worth (thanks to your poems),
but I still employ my pen to praise your name,
though I seem completely strange, unlike myself.

And as a plant absorbs, its leaves parched with thirst,
new liquor from the humid fertile earth,
and sends forth fruit and flowers despite its age,

so could I flower even now. This new thought
whispers in my heart, *take courage*,
from these examples, that I may yet bear fruit.

Ugolino Martelli a Tullia

Se, lodando di voi quel che palese
Di fuor si mostra a le piu strane genti,
Rare bellezze, & disusati accenti,
Degne parole a cio mi son contese;

Com'esser vi potrà larga, & cortese
La lingua a dir, che non tema o paventi
Di tante ascoste in voi virtuti ardenti,
Tullia, ch'amor divino al cor v'accese?

Bontà, senno, valor, & cortesia
Con l'altre mille insieme in voi cosparte
Rozamente contar forse potria;

Ma come rare, & eccellente sia
Ciascuna d'esse in voi con mille carte
Mantova, & Smirna a dir non basteria.

Tullia a Ugolino Martelli

Ben sono in me d'ogni virtute accese
Le voglie tutte, & gli spirti alto intenti;
Ma'l poter, & l'oprar si freddi, & spenti,
Ch'io mi veggo haver l'hore indarno spese.

Onde non lodi no; ma gravi offese
Mi son le rime nostre: & però tenti
Vostr'alto stil fra tante, & si eccellenti
Mille di lui cantar piu degne imprese.

Ben può celar il ver finta bugia:
A qualche tempo, o'n qualche loco, o parte:
Ma non si ch'ei no vinca, e'n sella stia.

Dunque pur secura, & corta via
Rivolgete UGOLIN tanta vostr'arte,
Ch'in altrui molto, in me poco saria.

Ugolino Martelli [84] to Tullia

If, praising all your qualities that show forth
to the far nations and peoples on the Earth,
beauties rare & accents seldom heard,
in appropriate and worthy words,

My claims would be contested, a scandal,
it would be; how can any tongue encompass
in words ineffable and courteous,
your many virtues, by divine love kindled?

Goodness, wisdom, valor and courtesy,
and a thousand more virtues in you dispersed;
I could only count them approximately.

But since each of them is rare and excellent,
a thousand pages would be insufficient
in the Latin of Mantua, of Smyrna, the Turk. [85]

Tullia to Ugolino Martelli

It is well and true, every virtue is aflame
in my spirits with desire, and high intent;
but the power to work is so cold and spent
that I see myself with hours spent in vain.

Not true praises, our poems offend me:
so please, no more: try UGOLINO,
your high style, among the many: praise our hero,
his thousand labors and his deeds so worthy.

We know a well-feigned lie can hide the truth
at any time or place, but in the battle
truth will win and remain in the saddle.

Therefore to be brief and to tell the truth,
UGO, turn to others your excessive art
for I need little, though others need a lot.

SELECTED PROSE

Muzio, Tullia's Lover, on His Muse, and
Tullia on the Pleasures of Reading

Dedication to
"La Tirrhenia del Mutio alla Signora Tullia d'Aragona"
From Muzio Iustinopolitano to Signora Tullia d'Aragona

Girolamo Muzio's pastoral eclogue "La Tirrhenia," which appeared in the 1547 edition of the Rime of Tullia d'Aragona, celebrates Tullia under the thin guise of the nymph La Tirrhenia. As he says in the dedication, included on the following pages, Muzio has endeavored in this work to paint a portrait — in words — of her soul. "La Tirrhenia" was one of nearly twenty poems Muzio composed in Tullia's honor.

The proper role for a lover, my most noble lady, is to desire to be always and entirely united with the beloved person; and even beyond that is the desire that I have for my soul to be indissolubly joined with yours — the desire that our names will be joined together and read together, and that they will live together in fame and immortality. And since your love has been a Helicon for me — an inspiration for my poetry — and you, a Muse bestowing favor upon me, it has lately occurred to me to create a new composition, containing more affection, perhaps, than artifice. That is to say, I am designing a more particular image of you, altogether different from those made by others I have seen up until now.[1] And if I do not have a hand so gifted so as to compose a true likeness, I thought to have at least sketched in the shadings of a portrait, like the shadows of heavenly beauties that draw our souls upward, ascending the ladder of the desire of true beauty: thus from this shadow of you made by me, the most noble spirits can ascend in the consideration of this truth that is you.[2] Now of that image, which I send to you, such as it is, I say nothing more, except that if any *figura*[3] can show — to corporeal eyes—that image which I have carried for a long time in my soul, and which I compare to you yourself, I am certain that you cannot discern whether it is drawn in you or in me, the truest image of the form conceived in the mind of God *ab eterno:* [4] the semblance Nature aspired to create when she wished to show what she was capable of down here on Earth.

To the Most Excellent Signora Tullia d'Aragona from Muzio Iustinopolitano

Muzio contributed the following as a prefatory statement to Tullia's Dialogo della infinità di amore, *published in Venice in 1547, the same year as the* Rime. *He played an important role in seeing the* Dialogo *into print, acting as her editor and literary agent; his publisher in Venice also published the* Rime *of Tullia d'Aragona.*

Noble valorous lady, just as the human being is composed of two parts, of which the one is terrestrial and the other celestial and eternal, so are there two kinds of beauties, as you know very well. And of these two, according to the nature of their parts, one is frail and transitory[5] and the other is living and immortal. Now, by means of these two splendors, of body and soul, we represent ourselves to others through the bodily senses, setting alight that desire which is called "love" in our hearts and souls. And yet these two splendors, being nothing other than that beauty of fancied bodily delight and that beauty illumined by the inner light of the soul, are the means by which everyone is drawn toward that object which is most desirable to him or to her. And as we have said, if the various kinds of beauty follow Nature in those parts of which She is the ornament, then it follows that such are the effects of the one and the other love. When the flower of our earthly garments [the body] diminishes with time, our earthly desires decrease; so inversely, the light of our souls burns more brightly—and for the one who once felt himself to be aflame, that flame grows greater day by day. Perhaps these things are not understood by everyone, but in those mature souls in whom other loving desires should already have come to an end, they are not lacking.

As one of those in this era who marvel at you, I wish to demonstrate that I love you no less than I have already for many years hence, contrary to the opinion of those who have perhaps damned me in their minds and held me as worthless. I want to tell them freely that not only do I love you no less than I loved you in the past, but I love you even more for the increase in you of that particular beauty which first induced me to love you, of which I am acutely conscious.

And, if they cannot discover this, it is because they do not see you with the same eyes with which I see you. For if they would seek a vision of you similar to my own, even a part of that vision with which I see you, then they would be aflame with love for you and they would praise me for my love as well. To me, your *Dialogue* has made a great demonstration of the increase of your beauty. It is futile to exhaust myself with regard to your writing, ornamenting your already-elegant writing with fitting praises, not appearing any more able to praise it than one who has been long in darkness. Such is your courtesy toward me, that since you are part of me, and your *Dialogue* is part of you, it is a worthy means of communication and not something that someone was compelled to publish. And — such is my love for you, that it has made me no less studious of your honor than of my own — that I will not be content until it sees the light.

And perhaps a particular desire for honor has driven me thus far: understanding that I love high beauty (inner as well as outer), I am sure that I will be honored and praised by the noblest spirits for producing something so glorious. Great is the assurance that Love brings to the one who truly loves. Not only did I desire to publish this work of yours without your knowledge, but I desired to go further. You introduce a dialogue among yourself, Varchi, and Dr. Benucci,[6] in which so many things are said in praise of you and of your virtue that it did not seem fitting to you to call yourself by your proper name; out of modesty you had called yourself "Sabina." Now, it did not seem right to me that in a dialogue a fictional name should occur between two real names; therefore, judging whether it should be all fiction or all truth, leaving your name thus changed would have done injury to your most noble spirit and to those who are pleased to live within your poems. These things being as they are, I have taken the liberty of putting the name "Tullia" in place of "Sabina." And that which I would not have done for another, I have done on such an occasion, pleased that Varchi, no less gifted than eloquent, makes honorable mention of me, as he does of you. And furthermore, I do not know that I have ever been in love with any Sabina, but I know full well that I always have belonged, and still belong, to Signora Tullia. And having said this, I am certain that the excellent Signor Speroni[7] would say it as well, upon hearing you so named. So I have taken the boldness to change this dialogue lest my censure fall upon another. My ardor is such that, having published your work, Love assures me that you will take it for a good thing, being none other than Love himself who has given me cause. Thus I hope that this book, published without your consent, should make you most happy. Before the composition was finished, and as such not yet worthy of true praise, you did not send it forth; you wanted to keep it hidden until it was ready. Yet I who have sent it forth should not be blamed, for I am certain that with your eternal fame and honor, the world will be in perpetual obligation to me for these labors.

Girolamo Muzio to Messer Antonio Mezzabarba

Tullia met Girolamo Muzio (1496–1576) at the Este court in Ferrara in 1537, where Muzio, a diplomat and man of letters, was in the service of Duke Ercole II. Tullia and Muzio were lovers, friends, and a source of inspiration for each other's work. In the following letter from Milan, dated 1550, Muzio answers a literary question with a personal anecdote, recalling how Tullia was a muse for him. The letter is addressed to the writer Antonio Mezzabarba, whom Muzio met in Dalmatia in 1513.

I have cherished the hope that these literary works of mine are sufficiently pleasing, as implied by your most kind letter to me. And because they are approved by a person of such good judgment, I will carry on, continuing to publish them with great eagerness of soul. And it would be taken by me as a great favor that a testimony so esteemed and honored as yours should be published; if your words should accompany my writings, it would bring to them the privilege of honor. By these words I might appear overly ambitious, perhaps — but you should not marvel at this. Stimulated by the zeal for honor, I have been cultivating my soul. If I have been laboring at this task and working toward that end, it is reasonable that I should want to taste the fruit of my desire. Not feeling myself capable of attaining such heights, however, and not having an adequate stairway by which to ascend, I would hope that my friends would help me, lifting me up on their shoulders and pushing me so that I may be able to attain the highest, uppermost branch. And by virtue of such faith I desire to receive help from you who love me so, as for the most part we are nourished from the same tree.

Hunger for honor and not power excuses me.

And passing on to your questions concerning my eclogue and to the intentions I have had in composing the part that is entitled "Furor": such was the occasion that I have been led to give it another name, that of "Disgrace." I will render the reason without recollecting my vanities. And speaking of first things first, I have for some time celebrated Signora Tullia under the name of Tirrhenia. Being with her one day and discussing these studies, in which she has taken so much delight and in which she still delights, we touched upon the subject of the Muses, their names and their virtues. Because things were such that we were somewhat in a state of furor,[8] because she herself had been gathering together this discourse almost as if she were recollecting a new thought, such as it were, and because that is the way it went, we took up the subject again. She said to me, "Already for many days I have had a concept in mind, and since now it occurs to me to propose it, I want to say: for a long time, you have celebrated me in song under the name of Tirrhenia; now I would like you to change my name and call me Thalia,[9] but I would like you to do it in a such a way that it is obvious that Thalia and Tirrhenia are the same person, that you have now thought of it this way." I responded that I would do it.

We were in Ferrara, and between the rooms of her apartments and mine, there was a remote and out-of-the-way place in the middle, spacious enough so that I stopped to take a walk and to think. By the time I left, therefore, I found a way to accommodate my intentions, and thus I began the composition. And I felt so moved by the subject that the following day (at the very hour in which we parted the day before) I returned to her with the finished product, as she would testify, as memory yet serves and recounts, and as it has been confided to diverse friends. And I swear on my faith that in the form in which I brought it to her at the hour of this composition, I believe that I had not put fifteen verses in order — and now they are closer to two hundred. The plot was that Mopso was so transported by furor that one night that he found himself in Helicon,[10] where he realized that he was with the one whom he loved in the form of a nymph — and that it was Thalia. And there, she and Erato[11] gathered him up, crowned him, and refreshed him, giving him Hippocrene water[12] to drink. Then, in imitation of Horace, I wrote that he was transformed into a swan and ascended to the circle of the moon.[13] I wrote this because Thalia was represented by the harmony of this sphere, and the sphere infused her with virtue; according to the following eclogue, I declare that each of the Muses is assigned her own particular realm of heaven. I know that Thalia should be signified by the color green (which, as you know, is taken from the Greek verb for the process of growth and renewal).[14] Just so, she renews the wit of those she graces with her favors, making them young and green again. And, by having given myself the name of Mopso, giving the eclogue the name of Tirrhenia for a title, I was greatly contented to have felt the furor that had taken hold of me in writing this composition. This was also the reason for making me add a verse, having in the beginning said to her,

>   And while I played my flute,
>   you lent your ears to the furor of your Mopso.

Then I added,

>   And in the furor of Mopso, my own furor.

And this was my reason for writing this eclogue; this, my subject; this, my intention. And since we have entered upon this subject of the Muses, I want to add another thing to this proposition. Virgil, in one of his invocations, says,

> You or Calliope while I sing
> Grant me, I pray, your favor.

Upon which point the grammarians became confused, wanting to accord the pronoun "you" to Calliope, and Calliope to the verb *porgete*, grant this not being the Latin form of speech. But in my eclogue, the true interpretation is drawn from the one who is entitled Thalia, that is to say, Thalia being the sound of the heaven of the Moon, Euterpe of Mercury, Erato of Venus, Melpomene of the Sun, Clio of Mars, Terpsichore of Jupiter, Polyhymnia of Saturn, and Uranus of the starry heaven; and Calliope being that concentric circle which is formed from those other eight spheres, Virgil learnedly and lightly joins the two pronouns as *Voi* and assigns the verb *porgete* to Calliope, being the one that comprises so many together, using the figure of speech that is most often used in those nouns called "collective" in Latin. This is my opinion of that theme, or *topos*, as he interprets it, and now that it returns to my memory, it does not seem to me irrelevant to say these few words.

I come now to the Disgrace, of which I will not make such a long discourse. During the course of my love with Signora Tullia, the Duke of Ferrara, whom I served until now, sent me to Milan for his affairs. From there, having written her a few letters, but with responses not forthcoming, I dedicated myself, full of regret, to the composition of this eclogue. And being on the point of quarreling, I finally had three letters from her at once, whereby the occasion to lament further ceased, and since many things remained unsaid, I finished the composition. And because I wanted to show that our quarrel had been mended, I decided to weave together the strands of life and art. Since that part of the eclogue had been written first, before the concept in my mind recalled and changed it, I thought that I should give it the name of "Disgrace."

In sum, I have stated my intentions and the cause of the "Furor" and of the "Disgrace": those things that have been so true that they needed to be declared. And if others have wanted to discuss it without knowing the whys and the wherefores, it is because they have wanted to believe things that are so far from all truth, like many things one hears about the poems of Petrarch, of which no one knows the basis of their subjects.

From Milan

To the Readers of

Il Meschino Altramente detto il Guerrino,

written in Ottava Rima by Tullia d'Aragona, a work in
which the principal parts of all the world are seen and
understood, and many other delightful things to be greatly
prized by every person of good and prudent judgment. [15]

Tullia's chivalric epic, Il Meschino altramente detto il Guerrino *(The lit-*
tle wretched one, otherwise known as the little warrior), was published posthumously
in 1560. The preface "To the Readers" that accompanies the epic, included on the
following pages, exalts the pleasures of reading and denigrates the corrupting influ-
ence of books with lewd themes, for reasons that will become apparent. Tullia
d'Aragona's claim of taking an original prose narrative and recasting it into ottava
rime *verse is true: she chose a prose narrative, Andrea da Barberino's* Meschino
decto Guerrino, *and "translated" it into the verse form of* ottava rima. Il
Meschino *is comparable to the* Orlando Furioso *in form, length, and plot, fea-*
tures of the epic genre that were hotly debated in Italy in the Cinquecento.

Of all the honorable and delightful pastimes available to human
beings, nothing is so useful and so dear as having something
uplifting and pleasant to read, as experience clearly demonstrates.
For almost all other pastimes require the assistance of others — we
cannot have access to them continuously, neither when nor how we
wish. Furthermore, such entertainments such as eating and drinking
and so forth, may soon become tiresome and tedious; sometimes
they are dangerous, or mentally laborious, or expensive; and they
often produce harmful or displeasing results. Such is the case with
gadding about, with gaming, with love affairs, and with many other
such things that are not fitting to discuss here at length. With read-
ing, however, it is otherwise: we can manage it ourselves, according
to our own will; we can do so whether alone or accompanied by oth-
ers; a lot or a little; without expense, without peril, without harmful
consequences, without anxiety, but rather with an end result of great

contentment and satisfaction. And if this singularly perfect solace, this great elevation of the spirit is universally accessible, shared by every man and every woman not completely base and vile in spirit, then it is much more useful and necessary to women—as Giovanni Boccaccio knew very well, declaring as much in the preface to his *Decameron*.[16] There, he demonstrates at length how he applied himself to the task of writing this work almost entirely for the uplifting of women alone. He can be faulted on only one count: would that he had only known well enough to choose to do one very important thing, and to avoid another. There is no doubt that he would have been worthy of the highest praise, if only he had taken his own advice and fully carried out his intention to create something truly noble, something that could be appreciated by true ladies—with respect to them, and to himself, as well as with respect to other men who are honest and noble in spirit. The first thing that he neglected to do was to write in verse, which one reads, without a doubt, with much more pleasure than one does prose—so much more effectively does it make an impression upon our souls, and leaves its form upon our memories with such pleasure.[17] The other thing that he did not know to do, or perhaps did not elect to do— either by a great imperfection of judgment or due to an imperfection in his nature—was to avoid putting so many truly filthy, dishonorable, and wicked things into his work. And one can see them throughout his book, from one end to the other, unapologetically and without regard for the honor of married women, or widows, or nuns, or secular virgins, or godmothers, or godfathers, or friends among themselves, or priests, or monks, or finally even prelates, or Christ, or God himself. Can one gain fame and glory from such writings, from such filthy *novelle* and from so many wicked words, and thus treat Christ, so as to put horns on his head and on the heads of many others besides? It is truly astonishing how not only princes and noblemen, but even thieves and traitors who call themselves Christians nevertheless behave in such a way, but even they have never permitted themselves to hear the name [of Boccaccio] without making the sign of the cross and covering their ears, as one would do upon hearing the most atrocious, horrendous, and wicked thing that human ears could hear. But our nature is so corrupt that not only do we not flee from such a thing as from an abomination, but we run to it: the book is so much in demand, so desired by everyone, and has risen in such esteem that they have called him the father of the language, the Tuscan Cicero. And finally even LUDOVICO DOLCE,[18] GIROLAMO RUSCELLI,[19] and my own PIETRO BEMBO,[20] and many others of the most rare intellect have been moved to proclaim him a classic, to explicate him, to declare him famous, and to exalt him above the seven heavens. Therefore it is no wonder if, ambitious to attain the same kind of glory, others have undertaken the task of creating Nannas and Pippas and Errant Prostitutes, and most recently, that book which has most certainly offended the majesty of the most noble city of Siena, clearly based upon those who were born and raised there.[21] Therefore, having had from my earliest years more knowledge of the world than I would wish to have had, and now having acquired more wisdom than before, I have seen in myself as well as in many others how much harm there is in the discussion[22] and in the reading of ugly and lascivious things. On the other hand, knowing how much women — and men — are ardently desirous to read and hear delightful and pleasing things, I spent some time researching almost all the books of history and poetry that our language has to offer. Therefore, as I have said, I resolved that poetry, in many respects and principally in that of verse, is more appreciated by everyone than all the other forms. Yet I found that epics such as *Morgante*,[23] *Ancroia*,[24] *Orlando Innamorato*,[25] *Bovi d'Antona*,[26] *Leandra*, the *Mambriano*,[27] and finally those of Ariosto[28] himself do not lack the great vice of containing such lascivious, shameful, and unworthy things, not only unsuitable for nuns, young women, widows, or married women — but even for public women, if they should happen to see them by chance (for, after all, it is not a new thing that a woman, by necessity or through some other malevolent fortune that might befall her, should happen to fall into corporeal error and appear to be unfitting, shameful, and indecorous in her speech and in other things, although perhaps appearing more so to others than to herself).[29] Therefore, I say, it was my constant and most fervent desire to find some delightful and pleasant book to read in which shameful and ugly things are not to be found. And so, after having pored over all the books that I could acquire, I finally discovered this very lovely book in the Spanish language in which so many and such varied things are to be found—that I know of no other existing book in any language that is more pleasing and more joyful in its essence.[30] And then it was also so completely chaste, so pure, and so Christian that neither in word, nor example, nor in any other manner could it be considered objectionable; rather, it is a work that any honorable and holy man, any married woman, virgin, widow, or nun could read at any time. Therefore, from beginning to end, it is obvious that the author of this book had thought to draw out the souls of women (as well as honest, just, and holy men) with elegance, with sweetness, and with the greatest delight. But this book was missing the most important prerequisite for literary perfection, which is, as I mentioned earlier, the pleasing elegance of verse, as it had been written in prose. And seeing that, I set about to do something useful and gracious in the world, if possible, and render it into verse myself. Considering and understanding the popularity of these books written in *ottava rima*, I have learned about the diversity of styles from many people of prudent judgment.[31] As we have just seen, some go slithering along the earth on their bellies, so that every soul not completely vile in nature disdains even to see them, let alone to find delight in reading them.[32] One encounters others who, having aspired to please almost exclusively the learned, have lifted themselves up so much, that not only average readers—and principally women readers—but even the learned themselves also have great difficulty in many places, in understanding the books. Authors and scholars have trouble making the books accessible, resulting in an endless stream of commentaries and textual explications, as with works of law or philosophy. Therefore, I have sought to remain among those who have followed the middle way, like Pulci principally,[33] and Boiardo, and the author of the *Mambriano*. According to my criteria, these works have not yet endured the test of time insofar as style is concerned, but they offer utility, accessibility, and the added charm of delight.[34] In language, then, I have chosen to follow the dialect not of one sole province, but of all of our Italy, and that diction which is employed by the most illustrious and judicious persons. In this respect I have always valued the opinion, the counsel, and the aid of as many prudent and learned people as possible. With the sincere and freely given advice of such intellects, I am confident of having endeavored to give the world a book that is most gracious in every part, one that may be read with full delight and utility by every sort of person of honest and good will. I desire and hope that your task, most noble spirits, will be to accept only my good intentions and to give all praise to God alone, the source of every good thing and the one to whom I give thanks for this great grace: that at an age not yet overly mature but youthful and fresh, I have been given the light with which to commend myself to Him with my whole heart and to desire and exhort others — men equally as well as women — to do the same, as much as is in my power.

ENDNOTES

Notes to the Translator's Preface of the 2006 Edition of Tullia d'Aragona Rime *and to the Introduction, pages 11–30.*

1. *Rime della Signora Tullia di Aragona et di diversi a lei* (Venice: Gabriel Giolito de' Ferrari et Fratelli, 1547; reprinted 1549, 1560); (Naples: Antonio Bulifon, 1693).

2. *Le rime di Tullia d'Aragona: Cortigiana del secolo XVI,* ed. Enrico Celani (Bologna: G. Romagnoli, 1891; Bologna: Commissione per i testi di lingua, 1968).

3. The Italian transcriptions in this book follow the 1547 first edition of the *Rime della Signora Tullia d'Aragona et di diversi a lei* rather than the rearranged and heavily edited edition of 1891. Apart from a very few instances in which obvious errors were corrected, this book more closely follows the first (1547) edition rather than the "newly edited and corrected" posthumous edition of 1560, in which judgment calls made by the editor substantially altered the text. Thanks once more to the generous and helpful library staff at the Biblioteca Nazionale Centrale di Firenze for access to the first and second editions.

4. Ann Rosalind Jones, "Bad Press: Modern Editors Versus Early Modern Women Poets (Tullia d'Aragona, Gaspara Stampa, Veronica Franco)," in *Strong Voices, Weak History: Early Women Writers & Canons in England, France, & Italy,* eds. Pamela Joseph Benson and Victoria Kirkham (Ann Arbor: University of Michigan Press, 2005), 287, 295.

5. "Dialogo della Signora Tullia d'Aragona della infinità di amore," in *Trattatisti del Cinquecento,* ed. Mario Pozzi (Bari: Laterza, 1978), 201; *Dialogue on the Infinity of Love,* trans. Rinaldina Russell and Bruce Merry (Chicago: University of Chicago Press, 1997), 69.

6. The phrase "subject of desire" is borrowed from Deborah Lesko Baker, *Subject of Desire: Petrarchan Poetics and the Female Voice in Louise Labé* (Purdue UP, 1996).

7. John Locke, *An Essay Concerning Human Understanding,* Bk .3, Ch. 1, section 2. Ed. Jack Lynch http://andromeda.rutgers.edu/~jlynch/Texts/locke-language.html: "Besides articulate sounds, therefore, it was further necessary that he should be able to use these sounds as signs of internal conceptions; and to make them stand as marks for the ideas within his own mind, whereby they might be made known to others, and the thoughts of men's minds be conveyed from one to another."

8. Similarly, Jeanette Winterson argues that one should resist reading biographical assumptions into literature: "A writer's work is not a chart of their sex, sexuality, sanity, and physical health." In another essay, she states: "I am a writer who happens to love women. I am not a lesbian who happens to write." See her *Art*

Objects (New York: Vintage International, 1997), 97, 104. Similarly, Tullia d'Aragona was a poet who happened to have been a courtesan, not a courtesan who dallied with poetry.

9. Unfortunately, in many places in the world in which human trafficking is practiced, this is still the case. For statistics, information, and a brief description of programs attempting to combat this present-day form of human slavery: http://www.unfpa.org/swp/2003/english/ch2/page4.htm.

10. Noted for her rhetorical elegance, *Tullia* was compared with Marco *Tullio* Cicero (Latin, Marcus Tullius) by two contemporaries, Niccolò Martelli and Battista Stambellino. Enrico Celani remarks: "Thanks to the affection of her father, she was able to write and argue in Latin, things worthy of any great *letterato* [man of letters] . . . adding to her wisdom and virtue a refined and delicate manner. [. . .]" *Rime di Tullia d'Aragona,* (1891), viii, xxii–xxxiii. Salvatore Rosati claims that she was celebrated for her *bella voce* (beautiful voice) as well as for her erudition. See *Tullia d'Aragona* (Milan: Treves Editori: 1936), 12, 46.

11. Salvatore Bongi cites the letter mentioning her "excellentissima" eloquence and knowledge of every thing." See *Annali di Giolito* (Rome: Presso i Principali Librai, 1890), 167, 170.

12. The "modesty *topos*" is especially frequent in the first fourteen poems of the *Rime,* addressed mostly to members the Medici family; the next twenty-four are addressed to various *literati* (friends and supporters who are poets, humanists, diplomats, clergymen, etc.)

13. The phrase "self-fashioning" is associated with Stephen Greenblatt. See *Renaissance Self-Fashioning: From More to Shakespeare* (Chicago: University of Chicago Press, 2005); for the philosophical basis of the concept, see *on the Dignity of Man* (*Oratio De Dignitate hominis,* 1486) by Pico della Mirandola (1463–1494). Cf. Pico Project at Brown University: http://www.brown.edu/Departments/Italian_Studies/pico/>.

14. Thalia is the muse of comedy and pastoral poetry. Her symbols are the mask of comedy and the shepherd's crook. For the Helicon reference, see poem VI, above.

15. For details on this Renaissance "best-seller," see Ann Moss, *Latin Commentaries on Ovid from the Renaissance* (Signal Mountain, TN: Summertown, 1999), 29.

16. For the myth of Philomela, see Ovid, *Metamorphoses,* Book VI, lines 424–674.

17. For the tale of Cupid and Psyche, see Lucius Apuleius, *The Golden Ass,* trans. Jack Lindsay (Bloomington: Indiana University Press, 1962), Books IV–VI. See especially the passages dealing with Psyche's descent, or *katabasis,* VI. 17–21 and her final, triumphant transformation, VI. 23.

18. For a more detailed analysis of the polemic between Tullia d'Aragona and Bernardino Ochino with reference to poem XXV, see "The Poet as Salome," pages 23–29 of *Sweet Fire,* above.

19. See Rosati's *Tullia d'Aragona,* 163–67, for information on Piero Manelli, even though Rosati, reads the masterful poem XXVIII too biographically. Striking a rhetorical balance between body and soul, heaven and earth, form and matter, Tullia d'Aragona challenges Manelli, as a male poet, to think of her as a spiri-

tual equal, quite unthinkable in 1546. Furthermore, it seems that she also is addressing future readers and even hoping for poetic immortality, the desire to live through her work when her soul is separated from the "veil of her body". For an analysis of the sestina that concludes the first section of the *Rime*, see Elizabeth A. Pallitto, "Apocalypse and/or Metamorphosis: Chronographia and Topographia in Petrarch's Sestina XXII and Tullia d'Aragona's Sestina LV" in *Comitatus: A Journal of Medieval and Renaissance Studies*, Vol. 33 (2002), 59–76. (In the 1547 *Rime*, the sestina is not LV but XXXVIII).

20. Some nineteenth-century scholars believe that Tullia's father was the archbishop of Palermo, Pietro Tagliavia d'Aragona. See Bongi, *Annali*, 152–54; and Celani, *Rime*, xix, note 5. Recent research, however, supports the hypothesis that Tullia's father was Luigi d'Aragona, a cardinal under Pope Alessandro VI. Bongi claims the young cardinal frequented Giulia, who gave birth to a daughter, and provided for her regally (152). While allowing for the possibility that Giulia lied, Rosati (11) still finds Luigi's paternity plausible, quaintly attributing Tullia's poetic talent to her *sangue reale* (royal blood).

21. For at least a decade, Luigi d'Aragona lived with Tullia's mother and supported her. (See Celani, xx, n. 1.). Hypothetically, Luigi is the son of Enrico "marchese di Gerace," the illegitimate son of Ferdinand of Aragón by his concubine Diana Guardato (Celani, xix, note). See also Bongi, *Annali* (Rome, 1890), 152; footnote, 153. Domenico Zanrè explains the relationships thus: "Tullia's father was allegedly Cardinal Luigi d'Aragona, the illegitimate grandson of King Ferdinand I of Aragón and Naples. Giulia was at the peak of her profession in 1508, and having a liaison with the twenty-nine-year-old Luigi. The relationship is believed to have lasted from 1505 until 1515 and perhaps even longer." Zanrè, *Cultural Non-Conformity*, 146; see also Basile, 140, *op.cit.*, note 17 above. Ferdinand's title changes upon the acquisition of new realms, a source of potential confusion. In 1468, Ferdinand became King Ferdinand II of Sicily; in 1469, he married Isabella I of Castile, uniting Aragón and Castile; in 1474, he became King Ferdinand II of Aragón; in 1479, he became King Ferdinand V of Castile and León; and in 1504, King Ferdinand III of Naples.

22. Rosati, 46.

23. For the hypothesis that Penelope is Tullia's daughter, see Bongi, *Annali*, 161; Zanrè, *Cultural Non-Conformity*, 146.

24. "Penelope died at thirteen years and eleven months in February of 1549 and was buried in the church of S. Agostino with an inscription marked Penelope Aragona." (Celani, xxix).

25. Tullia d'Aragona may have blamed her mother for corrupting her, as does her biographer Rosati. Rosati claims that Giulia's greed and bad counsel may have caused the scandal that forced them to leave Rome: her efforts to "sell" Tullia for a phenomenal price to a repulsive German named Gianni. See his *Tullia d'Aragona*, 59–60.

26. *Rime della S. Tullia di Aragona et di diversi a lei. Nuovamente corrette et ristampate.* (Venice: Giolito, 1560), 42. I cite the more readily available second printing. In this son-

net, the comparison in favor of Tullia over Vittoria Colonna must have ruffled the feathers of Colonna, in many ways Tullia's antithesis: a widow with Protestant sympathies and ties to Bernardino Ochino. See the polemical poem XXV by Tullia "to the preacher Ochino."

27. "... La Signora Tullia Aragona feciono et esser volsono libera, esempta et immune dall'osservantia della legge soprascritta ... in l'avvenire ella possa et gli sia lecita, et così in virtù del presente partito et deliberatione gli permessono el portare quelli vestimenti habiti et ornamenti che gli parrà et piacerà." ([The office of the Magistrates] has declared Mme. Tullia "free, exempt, and immune from the observation of the above-mentioned laws ... and in the future, by virtue and by the deliberation of those present she may legally wear the garments and ornaments that are ... pleasing to her). (Zanrè, 171).

28. Virginia Cox, "Sixteenth-Century Women Petrarchists and the Legacy of Laura," in *The Journal of Medieval and Early Modern Studies* 35 (2005), 583–606.

29. See pages 99–103 of *Sweet Fire*, above.

30. The quotation from the "Proemio" of Boccaccio's *Decameron* reads as follows: "And though my support or comfort, so to say, may be of little avail to the needy, nevertheless it seems to me meet to offer it most readily where the need is most apparent, [...] Who will deny, that it should be given, for all that it may be worth, to gentle ladies much rather than to men? Within their soft bosoms, betwixt fear and shame, they harbour secret fires of love, and how much of strength concealment adds to those fires, they know who have proved it. Moreover, restrained by the will, the caprice, the commandment of fathers, mothers, brothers, and husbands, confined most part of their time within the narrow compass of their chambers, they live, so to say, a life of vacant ease, and, yearning and renouncing in the same moment, meditate divers matters which cannot all be cheerful." www.stg.brown.edu/projects/decameron/engDecShow Text.php?myID=proem&expand

31. In English, the passage reads as follows: "Prostitutes may not wear clothing of tapestry or silk, but jewels are permitted, gold and silver as much as they want, and they are held to the restriction of wearing on their heads either a veil of yellow silk or another similar material, so that it is visible by everyone, thus the purpose of this sign is so that they are distinguishable from respectable ladies whose lives are honorable, facing the penalty, if they neglect to wear the veil, of 10 *scudi* of gold for each time that they transgress." See Bongi, *Annali di Gabriel Giolito*, 183. Note that while the courtesan's veil can be made of silk, her clothes may not be composed of such rich material.

32. For the "affair of the veil" see Deana Basile, "*Fasseli gratia per poetessa*: Duke Cosimo I de' Medici's Role in the Florentine Literary Circle of Tullia d'Aragona" in *The Cultural Politics of Duke Cosimo I de' Medici*, ed. Konrad Eisenbichler (Aldershot: Ashgate, 2001), 135–147.

33. The treatise on love is *Il Dialogo della Signora Tullia d'Aragona della infinità di amore* (Venice: Gabriel Giolito de' Ferrari, 1547); cf. *The Dialogue on the Infinity of Love*, ed. and trans. Rinaldina Russell and Bruce Merry (University of Chicago Press,

1997). Tullia's poetry (and poems composed in her honor) first appear in *Rime della Signora Tullia di Aragona et di diversi a lei* (Venice: Gabriel Giolito de' Ferrari, 1547).

34. The letter of exemption from Cosimo contains the phrase "Fasseli gratia per poetessa" (give her grace for she is a poet) written in his hand. The letter is reproduced in an appendix in *Cultural Non-Conformity in Early Modern Florence* by Domenico Zanrè (Aldershot: Ashgate, 2004), 170–171. See also Deana Basile, *"Fasseli gratia...", op.cit.*

35. See Ann Rosalind Jones, *The Currency of Eros: Women's Love Lyric in Europe, 1540–1620*, 104; Zanrè, *Cultural Non-Conformity*, 166.

36. Basile, 142; see also Zanrè, 166.

37. Basile, 142.

38. Basile, 141. 1; Zanrè, 37.

39. "La Tullia, il Varchi, ed Ugolino e lei/Hanno fatto lega, e studian tutta la notte/E voglion pur che i ranocchi sian botte/E che gli etruschi non siano aramei." Basile, 143–44.

40. Zanrè, 146.

41. Zanrè, 147.

42. Sperone Speroni, *I Dialoghi di Messer Sperone Speroni* (Venice: Aldus Manutius, l542).

43. This rewritten Tullia character appears in the *Dialogo della Signora Tullia d'Aragona della infinità di amore* (Venice: Giolito, 1547); *Dialogue on the Infinity of Love*, tr. Rinaldina Russell and Bruce Merry (Chicago: University of Chicago Press, 1997).

44. Jones, *The Currency of Eros*, 103–117, especially 104–5; Zanrè, 164–67.

45. In an article entitled "Bad Press: Modern Editors versus Early Modern Women Poets (Tullia d'Aragona, Gaspara Stampa, Veronica Franco)," Ann Rosalind Jones questions Guido Biagi's assumption that the painting is a portrait of Tullia d'Aragona. In *Strong Voices, Weak History*, ed. Benson and Kirkham, *op. cit.*, 294.

46. Quoting Pier Virgilio Begni Redona's citation of Biagi: "la grazia raffaelesca sposata al vigoro *colorire* dei veneziani [...]." (*Colorito*, the delicate, light-inflected use of color was a trademark of Titian and the Venetian school). In *Alessandro Bonvicino, il Moretto* (Brescia: La Scuola, 1988), 354–355 (portrait, plate 79).

47. "The painting first belonged to a convent of nuns [...] the [designation] Erodiade is nothing but a pious lie of those nuns, to be able to register it [...] in sacred history, hiding something celebrated in profane history under another thing." "Nothing in the painting," he adds, would imply "the vindictive mother of Salome." Redona, 354. Translation mine.

48. *Ibid.*, 355.

49. Guido Biagi, *Tullia d'Aragona: Un' Etèra Romana* (Florence: Roberto Paggi, 1897), 3–5. For recent scholarship on the depiction of other Old Testament heroines such as Judith and Susanna, see Mary D. Garrard, *Artemisia Gentileschi: The Image of the Female Hero in Italian Baroque Art* (Princeton: Princeton University Press, 1989). See also *The Artemisia Files: Artemisia Gentileschi for Feminists and Other Thinking People*, ed. Mieke Bal (Chicago and London: University of Chicago Press, 2005).

50. The laurel leaves in the background can be seen in a similar portrait by

Giorgione, *Laura*, Jaynie Anderson, "The Giorgionesque Portrait: From Likeness to Allegory," in *Giorgione: Atti del Convegno Internazionale di Studio per il 5° Centenario della Nascita. 29–31 maggio 1978.* Comune di Castelfranco Veneto, l979.

51. Ann Rosalind Jones, "Bad Press," 294.
52. The story is found in the New Testament, Matthew 14.6–20 and Mark 6.14–25.
53. Celani, *Le Rime*, iv, note 1.
54. Thanks to Dr. Kevin McGinley for discussing these theological questions with me.
55. Girolamo Muzio, *Le mentite Ochiniane de Mutio Iustinapolitano* (Venice: Gabriel Giolito dei Ferrari et Fratelli, 1551; 1552). For Ochino's evangelistic leanings and correspondence, see Anne Jacobson Schutte, "The *Lettere Volgare* and the Crisis of Evangelism in Italy," *Renaissance Quarterly*, Vol. 28, No. 4 (Winter, 1975), 639–88.

Notes to Selections from the Rime by Tullia d'Aragona

1. Note on orthography: in the 1560 edition of the *Rime*, "Et" is created by intertwining the letters "E" and "t" into a calligraphic ampersand. Here, I have followed the original (albeit inconsistent) use of signifiers for "and": the ampersand, the Italian "e," and the Latin "et," all used in the 1547 edition. I have not duplicated the Latinate spellings of Italian that appear in the 1547 and 1560 editions: "v" instead of "u" and "j" instead of "i." As is customary in the period, a missing "m" or "n" is indicated by a tilde (~) in the original; here, the missing letters are inserted. In order to best reconstruct the original authorial choices, the following editions were consulted: 1547 Rime BNCF Palatino 2.5.3.29; 1560 Rime BNCF Palatino 2.5.3.30.

2. "Otio" is the Italian translation of the Latin "otium." Originally used as the opposite of "negotium" (days of business), "otium" implies days of leisure and pleasure. See note 11.

3. The "Consort" is Cosimo I de' Medici, whom Eleonora de Toledo married in 1539. (Here, the Spanish version of her name is used when discussing her as a member of the royal Spanish family of Aragón, in the text of the *Rime*, the Italian "*di* Toledo" is used).

4. A note of pride comes through in Tullia's otherwise "modest" dedication. See note 5.

5. The convention of the "modesty *topos*" is used in Renaissance prefaces and dedications, in which the poet protests, somewhat insincerely, his or her unworthiness. The term *sprezzatura* (effortless grace) is used to describe the downplaying of one's accomplishments. Ann Rosalind Jones comments on this pro forma "modesty" as an ironic understatement: "Tullia's humility toward the great is always double-edged, a way of elevating herself as poet at the same time that she insists on her indebtedness toward her addressees." Jones, *The Currency of Eros*, 105.

6. The first five poems are dedicated to Cosimo I de' Medici (1519–1574), Duke of Florence (1537–69) and Grand Duke of Tuscany (1569–74).

7. The octave, with its imagery of nymphs, shepherds, and Pan (a pagan god asso-

ciated with chaos and desire) contrasts with the sestet, in which the poet offers her gift of verse to Cosimo I, balancing pastoral conceit and courtly praise.

8. Again, Ann Rosalind Jones provides a gloss on what would otherwise sound like a bizarre ritual: "Recalling the garlands and incense that ancient shepherds took to Pan's temples [...] his own breast and heart must replace the temples, and her soul must be her offering to him" (in the form of poetry). See Jones, 105.

9. Cosimo I de' Medici was not quite eighteen when he took power in 1537.

10. In the Renaissance, individual man was considered a *cosmos* (world) in himself; Cosimo's name lends itself to this conceit, expressed here with particular grace.

11. The Roman king Numa Pompilius built the temple of Janus, established the twelve lunar months, and declared days of *otium* (rest) as opposed to *negotium* (business). See note 2. See Christopher Hibbert, *Rome: The Biography of a City* (London: Penguin, 1985), 5. Cosimo, then, is the "new Tuscan Numa."

12. The Arno flows through Florence, while the Arbia is associated with Siena. As the poet is beset by legal troubles in Siena (where political troubles also abounded), her haven is the Medici court in Florence. As in classical poetry, the *genius loci*, or spirit of the place, are symbolized by the rivers.

13. The poet, not yet confident as a courtier, modestly protests her unworthiness, asking only to be welcomed into the court as a sort of flute-girl, or rustic entertainer.

14. A stylized lily (the *fleur-de-lis*) was the symbol of Florence.

15. Helicon in Boeotia was thought to be the "home" of the Muses (Greek goddesses of poetry and song). Their mother is Mnemosyne (Memory), who was impregnated by Zeus.

16. Because Cosimo is such a benevolent patron of the arts, the Muses leave their normal home on Mount Helicon, in favor of the Arno (Florence) and the Medici court.

17. The Capricorn *impresa* or insignia (a half-goat, half-fish figure) appears in many works of sculpture, painting, and architecture honoring Cosimo, Eleonora, and her family. A statue of Apollo created by Domenico Poggini created for the garden of Don Luigi de Toledo depicts a *capricorno*, with the following inscription: FLOR ARTIFEX F. MDLIX; Poggini wrote a poem to accompany the sculpture. Later printed by Rucellai in *Impresa* (Venice, 1584), the poem is oddly reminiscent of Tullia d'Aragona's *Rime* to Cosimo.

> Benfu grande, e pregiato il tuo valore
> O, sacro *Apollo* contra l'empia fera,
> Che gir ne fe tua chiara fronte altera
> Tolto a i mortali un se tremendo orrore.
>
> E quel, che già ti punse, e passò il core
> Dorato stral, di che per la riviera
> Dafne seguisti a te si dolce, e fera
> Al cri ti riportò di Lauro onore.
> Or hai per terza Impresa altera, e nova

Coronato il celeste *Capricorno*
D'oro e di gemme, e di virtù fregiato.

Maggior' è 'l merto tuo, maggior la prova
Rendendo a chi 'l nemica, oltraggio e scorno,
Per farlo come in Terra, in Ciel Beato." [italics mine]

Great and prized was your valor, O sacred Apollo
when you fought against that impious beast
the Python. Turning your proud and famous brow,
you removed the horror that mortals feared most.

And that one who pierced you through the heart,
by the riverbank, wounding you so with a golden arrow
that you followed Daphne, that nymph fierce and sweet
until her honored laurel adorned your proud brow.

Now for your third labor, proud and new,
you have crowned heavenly Capricorn
with gold and gems as well as your virtue.

Greater is your merit, greater it will prove,
though you render to the enemy outrage and scorn,
make us who live on earth as blessed as those above.

The authors comment: "The artist, whose poetic powers even Vasari praised, here compares the Florentine Grande Duke to the Sun God [is] obviously projecting a glorification of his noble lord Cosimo I in the form of an Apollo which was to receive a prominent place in his palace or gardens. The *Capricorno* is the 'Impresa' of Cosimo I most frequently met with in Florence, since it was known that this symbol had also played a part in the horoscope of the Emperor Augustus, and the quiver denotes the young god, as does also the crown of laurels. In very much the same way Cosimo-Apollo appears in a medal by Poggini . . . an exact reproduction of our statue." The Italian poem and the quotation [translation mine] are taken from the following article: Ulrich Middeldorf and Friedrich Kriegbaum, "Forgotten Sculpture by Domenico Poggini," *The Burlington Magazine for Connoisseurs*, Vol. 53, No. 304 (July 1928), 8–13, 17.

18. Poems VIII–XI are addressed to Cosimo's noble Spanish wife Eleonora (1522–1562), who graced the Medici court with her nobility, wealth, and fecundity. See *The Cultural World of Eleonora di Toledo*, ed. Konrad Eisenbichler (Aldershot: Ashgate, 2004).

19. The Tagus (Spanish, *Tajo*; Portuguese, *Tejo*), is the major river of the Iberian Peninsula. It flows through Toledo and Aranjuez, Spain and Lisbon, Portugal, emptying into the Atlantic.

20. Tullia often uses the rhetorical device of antithesis. Here, beauty, traditionally and grammatically feminine (*la beltà*) is balanced with valor, gendered as masculine (*il valore*). *Donna* (lady) and *diva* (goddess) conflate Christian and classical imagery.

21. "Neither pen nor tongue" is a rhetorical device used in poetry to express ineffability.

22. See the image of the planet Venus in Dante's *Divina Commedia, Inferno* I, 37–40 (Milan: Mondadori, 1985) and also of Mars in Dante's *Purgatorio*, II, 10–24.

23. The angelic female figure in this poem evokes Dante's Beatrice (*Inferno*, II, 91–93): "I am made by God, his mercy such, that your misery does not touch me, nor do these flames assail me." It also evokes poem CVI of Petrarch's *Rime*: "Nova angeletta sovra l'ale accorta / scese dal cielo in su la fresca riva" (A new little angel on agile wings/came down from heaven to walk along the verdant riverbanks). Tullia's poem IX (and Petrarch's CVI) were echoed by Agnolo Bronzino in his use of the phrase "nuova angioletta" in a 1561 poem to Lucrezia de' Medici. On the Petrarchan iconography of the Medici court, see Gabrielle Langdon, "A 'Laura' for Cosimo: Bronzino's *Eleonora di Toledo with her son Giovanni*" in Eisenbichler, ed. *The Cultural World of Eleonora*, 49.

24. The speaker shifts from an earthly supplicant to a heavenly intercessory figure, but the poem is ambiguous. Although she is describing a woman, the angel's "gender" is masculine (*angeletto*). The "angeletto" could be Eleonora, the Virgin Mary, or neither.

25. On 5 July 1547, Cosimo and Eleonora had a boy, Don Garzia (1547–1562), one of nine surviving children. See Bruce Edelstein, "La Fecundissima Signora Duchessa," in Konrad Eisenbichler, *The Cultural World of Eleonora di Toledo*, 92; and Massimo Winspeare, *I Medici: L'Epoca Aurea del Collezionismo* (Livorno: sillabe s.r.l., 2001).

26. Maria Salviati de' Medici is the mother of Cosimo I. She died in 1543 (four years before the *Rime* were published), and is addressed in this poem as an angel in heaven. Benedetto Varchi, as a member of the Florentine Academy, delivered the funeral oration.

27. Don Luigi de Toledo (d. 1597) was Eleonora's brother; through her, he had access to the powerful Duke. The strong-willed Cosimo was nevertheless amenable to the influence of Eleonora and her relatives, who interceded on behalf of Tullia. If her father was Luigi d'Aragona, then Tullia would have been related to the house of Aragón.

28. The metaphor of the keys derives from the biblical account in which Jesus invests the apostle Peter with earthly power over heavenly matters. This image comes to symbolize the office of the Pope. "And to you I will give the keys of the kingdom of heaven...." (Matthew 16.18–19). With her extensive knowledge of her Italian poetic predecessors, Tullia is likely echoing Dante's *Inferno*, canto XIII, 58–60, where the same language is used by Pier' della Vigna to describe the power he had (and lost) to lock and unlock the heart of Emperor Frederick II of Sicily: "Io son colui che tenni ambo le chiavi / del cor di Federigo, e che

le volsi, / serrando e diserrando, sì soavi, / che dal secreto suo quasi ogn'uom tolsi" (I am the one who held both keys to the heart of Frederick, and turned them so softly, closing and opening, that I took from almost every man his secrets). Intertextual references are typical of Tullia d'Aragona's *Rime*.

29. Don Pedro of Toledo (1484–1553), Eleonora's nephew, was the Viceroy of Naples and the Marchese of Villafranca. As Viceroy, Don Pedro made civic advances and helped the city recover from the plague. In May of 1547, however, he almost caused an insurrection by trying to introduce the Spanish Inquisition into Naples, with disastrous results. The nobility and the populace united in opposition, and the more tolerant Roman Inquisition took over. Don Pedro frequented Tullia's salon (Zanrè, 147).

30. Parnassus is a mountain in central Greece, sacred to Mother Earth (and then to Apollo, the Muses, and Dionysus), from which the Castalian spring of poetic inspiration flowed. Cf. Dante: "Infino a qui l'un giogo di Parnaso / assai mi fu; ma or con amendue / m'è uopo intrar ne l'aringo rimaso" (Until now one peak of Parnassus sufficed for me, but now I need both, to enter into the arena that lies ahead). *Purgatorio*, II, 16–19.

31. Cf. Dante, *Purgatorio* I, 1–3: "Per correr migliori acque alza le vele / omai la navicella del mio ingegno, che lascia dietro a sé mar sì crudele" (To better sail the waters I now lift the sails of the little boat of my wit, that leaves behind a sea so cruel [inferno]).

32. Pietro Bembo (1470–1547) is a an important figure for Italian literature and language. Born in Venice, he studied under the Greek philosopher Constantine Lascaris (Costantino Lascaro) in Sicily. The printer and philologist Aldus Manutius also encouraged Bembo's interest in vernacular poetry, resulting in editions of Petrarch (*Cose volgari*, 1501) and of Dante (*Commedia*, 1502). Bembo's treatise *Prose della volgar lingua* (1525) codified Petrarchan poetry and helped to create a standard Italian language, a literary version of Tuscan that put the vernacular on the same lofty plane as Latin; his *Rime* served as a model for Petrarchan lyric in the Cinquecento. The 1535 edition of Bembo's *Rime* has a *proposta-risposta* format similar to Tullia's *Rime*; the 1530 edition does not. See Hairston, n. 36; see also William and Louise George Clubb, "Building a Lyric Canon: Gabriel Giolito and the Rival Anthologists" in *Italica*, Vol. 68, No. 3, (1991), 332–344. See also *Letteratura italiana, Le opere*, vol. 1, ed. Mirko Tavoni (Turin: Einaudi, 1992); *Prose e Rime*, ed. Carlo Dionisotti (Turin: UTET, 1966); Giulio Ferroni, *Storia della letteratura italiana: Dal Cinquecento al Settecento* (Milan: Einaudi, 1991), 93–96. The influence of printing also helped further the standardization and codification of the models in "Tuscan" dialect: Petrarch for poetry and Boccaccio for prose. For Tullia's position on Boccaccio as an exemplary model, see 100–101, below.

33. The Italian word *smarrita* (meaning lost or mislaid) has unmistakable echoes of Dante. In the *Inferno* (I, 3), the pilgrim is morally and spiritually "lost" in the "dark wood of error," the same sense in which Tullia uses the word.

34. Ridolfo Baglioni (1512–1533), captain of the Tuscan cavalry, played a signifi-

cant part in the history of Florence, leading pro-Medici forces to defeat the rebel army of Filippo and Piero Strozzi at Montemurlo in 1537. Filippo's capture and suicide marked a turning point in the establishment of Medici rule. See Zanrè, 8.

35. Tullia belongs to Apollo, the god of poetry; Baglioni belongs to Mars, the god of war.

36. Tullia's sojourn in Siena coincided with a period of grave political troubles there. Julia L. Hairston suggests that Crasso is Francesco Grasso, a Milanese nobleman elected in 1541 as Siena's Capitano di Giustizia. According to Hairston, Grasso "clashed with the ruling [party] in favor of the *Noveschi*, the political élite with which d'Aragona sympathized." See Hairston's article, "Out of the Archive: Four Newly-Identified Figures in the *Rime della Signora Tullia di Aragona et di diversi a lei* (1547)," *Modern Language Notes* Vol. 118, No. 1 (Jan. 2003), 257–63, 258. Siena's exiles were called *fuorusciti*; literally, "those who go out". While Tullia's allegiance to the ousted *noveschi* faction might have been problematic in Siena, it was an advantage in Florence. "By proclaiming her place among the imperial-backed Sienese refugees, d'Aragona took advantage of Cosimo's political stance and sought to ingratiate herself in Florence." Basile, 141.

37. This rhetorical device is called a *chiasmus*, after the Greek letter *x*; the antithesis is presented and then reversed, doubling back upon itself.

38. The wealthy Modenese poet Francesco Maria Molza (1489–1544) lived a large part of his life in Rome; he is known for his Latin and vernacular poetry. This poem must have been written when Molza was still alive, before the *Rime*'s publication. The mutual friend (called "noble soul") remains unknown.

39. "Colonello" Luca Antonio de Cuppis, or Cuppano (d. 1560), was a military colonel who fought for Cosimo's father, Giovanni delle Bande Nere. An expert soldier, he "spent virtually his entire life serving Cosimo both in town [Florence] as well as in Tuscany." Hairston, "Out of the Archive," 258; see note 36, above.

40. Ugolino Martelli (1519–1592) was an important figure in several of the Academies (intellectual societies that convened to study the classics and to write poetry in "the languages that mattered": Greek, Latin, and Tuscan). Their names were symbolic, humorous, or both: Accademia degli Intronati (the stunned), Accademia degli Infiammati (the enflamed, or burning ones), Accademia degli Umidi (the humid, or moist, as opposed to burning). Martelli first became associated with the Accademia degli Infiammati in Padua. Among the founders of the Accademia degli Umidi, also known as the Accademia Fiorentina, Martelli was also one of its most important members. Excellent sources on the academies are Richard S. Samuels, "Benedetto Varchi, the Accademia degli Infiammati, and the Origins of the Italian Academic Movement," *Renaissance Quarterly* Vol. 29, No. 4 (Winter 1976): 599–634, and Zanrè, *Cultural Non-Conformity.*

41. In the wood of the suicides (Dante's *Inferno*, XIII, 26–100), the pilgrim breaks off a branch that cries out, for it is a soul encased in a tree.

42. Writer and historian Benedetto Varchi (1504–1565) was born into an important Florentine family originally from Montevarchi. Having participated in the anti-Medici rebellion, he spent some time "in exile" in Padua and Bologna. At the invitation of Cosimo I, Varchi returned to Florence, where he became a member of the Accademia Fiorentina and an important figure in the literary affairs and religious reforms of the city. Varchi's *Storia fiorentina* narrates the history of Florence from the time of the republic, 1527–30, to 1537–38 (when Cosimo I established his power). For Tullia's letters to Varchi, see Zanrè, 169–71, and Bongi, *Annali di Giolito*, 184–86.

43. Arcadia, a Greek province in the central Peloponnese, joined the Achaean League in 244 B.C. In classical poetry, the adjective "arcadian" evokes an idyllic pastoral setting.

44. Varchi's political vicissitudes were largely of his own making. His decision to return to the court of Cosimo I and to discontinue his support of the losing republican (rebel) cause was largely pragmatic; he was welcomed by Cosimo as a sort of prodigal son when he returned to Florence. See Zanrè, 20.

45. The "minaccia morte" (menacing death) could be one of several perilous situations in which Tullia found herself in 1546: 1) the hostilities in Siena; 2) the decree of the veil; and 3), a difficult friendship with Ottaviano Tondi, one of the *Noveschi* elite who provoked the tumult of 1546 ("novesco provocatore del tumulto del 1546"). Accused of harboring Tondi as a fugitive, Tullia was under suspicion and her house was searched; although he was not found there, he was later tracked down and killed. Part of Tullia's interesting history with Tondi is the fact that his signature appears on the Decree (*Decreti*) in the affair of the yellow veil, either as an accuser or as an "accomplice." In *Shining Eyes, Cruel Fortune: The Lives and Loves of Italian Renaissance Women Poets* (New York: Fordham University Press, 2002), 79, Irma Jaffe suggests that he is both, speculating that Tullia became Tondi's lover in order to be released from the charges. Such a strategy would not have been an effective one, however; only the Duke could have pardoned her. Bongi surmises, plausibly, that Tondi would have been among the *entourage* accompanying her to church. (See *Annali di Giolito*, 176).

46. Girolamo Muzio (1496–1576), man of letters, diplomat, and courtier, was a close and extraordinarily supportive friend of Tullia's. Also known as Muzio Giustinapolitano (Latin, Mutio Iustinapolitano), after his father's place of origin, Muzio served at the courts of Pesaro, Urbino, and Ferrara. Like Tullia, whom he met at Ferrara, Muzio disagreed with Pietro Bembo on the "purity" and primacy of the Tuscan vernacular and argued for a synthesis of regional (especially northern) dialects. His works include *Eclogues*, poems published first in Tullia's *Rime* and again in 1550; his *dell'Arte Poetica* (On the art of poetry), published with *Rime Diverse* in 1551; *Le mentite Ochiniane* (Ochinian Lies) *del Mutio Iustinopolitano* (Venice: Giolito, 1551; 1552), note 49; and *Battaglie per la diffesa dell'italica lingua* (Battles for the defense of the Italian language), published posthumously. Tullia was a major source of inspiration for Muzio's poetry, as he was

for hers; he was also a source of the "infinite" love of which they both write. See Muzio's letter to Mezzabarba, pages 94–98 of *Sweet Fire*, above.

47. The phrase "antica fiamma," translated as "ancient flame," or former love, is an unmistakable echo of Dante when he is reunited in Paradise with his beloved Beatrice in *Purgatorio* XXX, 48: "conosco i segni dell'antica fiamma" ("I knew the signs of the ancient flame.") Tullia is Muzio's "ancient flame."

48. A river in northern Italy associated with the story of Francesca da Rimini and Paolo Malatesta, the tragic lovers whose story Dante tells in *Inferno*, V.

49. Bernardino Ochino (1487–1564) was a zealous preacher of repentance who upheld the doctrine of justification by faith (as opposed to works). Persecuted by the Roman Inquisition, Ochino fled Italy for Switzerland and England. In Geneva, he met John Calvin and converted to Calvinism, but the Calvinists eventually rejected him. Perhaps the Salome reference in the inscription on the painting (reproduced on the cover) refers to Ochino, whose views would have seemed extreme to the worldly court of Cosimo I.

50. This poem commemorates Emilio Tondi's brother Ottaviano, whose death Tullia mourns. Ottaviano was recorded among those who denounced her in Siena (Easter, 1544, and a second time later that year) for not wearing the yellow veil: "Die 23 augusti (1544). 'La Signora Tullia de Aragona per la pascha di Spirito Santo portò la sbernia contro li Statuti.'—Ottaviano Tondi, Horatio Pecci, Il Signor Gaspare servitore del Signor D. Giovanni." (R. *Archivio di Stato in Siena*, Decreti, polizze, ecc. del Capitano di Giustizia del 1544, luglio–dicembre, c. 53). Tullia's Sienese accusers may have been politically motivated. Cf. Celani, *Rime* (Bologna, 1891), note 37. See also notes 36 and 45, above.

51. The Roman Tiberio Nari is likely a previous acquaintance, as Tullia had not yet left for Rome in 1547. *Archivio Storico Capitolino*, cred. I, vol. 36, ff. 736–37; Pio Pecchiai, *Roma nel Cinquecento* (Bologna, 1948), 80–81. Quoted by Julia Hairston, "Out of the Archive," *MLN*, 258.

52. Piero di Lionardo Manelli (b. 1522) is an unusual interlocutor for Tullia. Unlike the other powerful men who were in a position to lend Tullia support, Manelli is neither known as a writer nor as a major player in Florence (or the other court cities of the Renaissance). Georgina Masson pieces together anecdotal evidence and speculates that the most passionate love poems among the *Rime*, XXVIII–XXXVI, are written with the young Manelli in mind, in *Courtesans of the Italian Renaissance* (New York: St. Martin's Press, 1975), 118. This poem stakes a claim for women artists (in response to Manelli's apparent views) and affirms Tullia's ambitions of immortality.

53. In Neoplatonic thought, the body is merely a veil for the soul. Tullia expresses this idea in a masterful sonnet of antitheses: body and soul, earth and heaven. Thus, the poem creates an image not only of the poet's desire to be remembered as a poet, but also of Renaissance thought. In formal terms, the poem is perfectly balanced.

54. Iconography of the pierced body of Jesus (or Saint Sebastian) was common in

the period; the poem also evokes Cupid, whose arrows "cause" poets to suffer, thereby providing them with subject matter. Cf. Petrarch, *Rime* poem V, and John 19.34: "One of the soldiers... plunged his spear into Jesus' side, and... blood and water poured out."

55. The story of Philomela is from Ovid's *Metamorphoses*, VI, lines 424–674. Tereus, seized by an overpowering lust for his sister-in-law Philomena, kidnaps her, imprisons her in a stone hut, rapes her, and cuts out her tongue. Philomena weaves a tapestry of the gruesome events and sends it to her sister Procne, Tereus's wife. In revenge, Procne kills their child, Itys, and feeds him to the child's father. Enraged, he tries to kill the sisters, but all three are turned into birds: Procne, into a swallow; Philomena, a nightingale; and Tereus, a hoopoe. In Renaissance poetry, Philomena is often merely associated with the coming of spring (See Jones, 115–16). Tullia's poem portrays a post-metamorphosis Philomena flying above the scene of the crime, triumphant, and—for a moment—happy.

56. The "Cyprian" means the goddess Venus, to whom the island of Cyprus is sacred.

57. Cupid's golden arrow was said to cause love; his lead arrow inspired disdain. For the story of Apollo and Daphne, see Ovid's *Metamorphoses*, Book I, 452–567.

58. The language of the last line is an echo of a letter from Muzio to Antonio Mezzabarba (1550): "Stimulated by the zeal for honor, I have been cultivating my soul.... It is reasonable that I should want to taste the fruit of my desire." The letter appears in this volume, pages 94–98.

59. The traditional combination of three figures—such as sailor, captain, and pilgrim—is a classical triad called the Virgilian *rota*. (Thanks to Blanford Parker, CUNY Graduate Center and Honors College, for reminding me of this). By including the figure of the mother, d'Aragona gives new meaning to an ancient theme, making a place for women.

60. The Sun is still used as a trope for the beloved in popular songs, such as "O Sole Mio."

61. The "free-hearted bird" of this poem is as essential to the speaker as the soul is to the body. In her *Dialogue*, Tullia integrates the roles of body and soul in love; here, body and soul represent the two (inseparable) lovers.

62. This poem takes standard tropes of Petrarch's love lyric—the hair as a net, the eyes as lights, the snow-white hand that holds the poet's heart, the beloved as the sun—and reworks them in a feminine voice. Also employed is the Latin elegiac construction *ubi sunt* ("where are..."). For the hand that holds the poet's heart in a murderous or loving embrace, see Petrarch's *Rime sparse*, XXXIII; in English, *Petrarch's Lyric Poems*, trans. and ed. Robert M. Durling (Cambridge, MA: Harvard University Press, 1976), XXXIII.

63. As suggested by line 5, Lilla may have been a pet, perhaps a little dog or a bird. It is known that Penelope, Tullia's "sister" (some say, daughter) had a pair of doves that died.

64. See note 37, above, on *chiasmus*.

65. In the myth, Psyche, forbidden from seeing her husband, Eros, steals a glimpse of him by candlelight one night while he sleeps. A drop of hot wax falls on him, revealing her lack of trust. As a punishment, Psyche and Eros are separated, and she is assigned impossible labors by the goddess Aphrodite. See Apuleius, *Metamorphoses*, IV, 28–35, V, VI, 1–24. The labor that renders one "breathless" might be the act of singing (or writing poetry). The translation of this poem is dedicated to the memory of William.

66. In Neoplatonic philosophy, the soul's truth is not visible or manifest to the senses.

67. The phrase "second death," used in a Christian context, could be referring to the death or damnation of the soul after the death of the body. Here it seems to mean suffering on Earth, i.e., in the imperfect realm of matter.

68. The metaphor of the salamander was used by the poets of the *scuola siciliana* (Sicilian school). According to legend, the salamander was said to be able to live in fire; in poetry, this is used to signify the ability to live with a "consuming" passion.

69. The oxymoron "sweet fire" (*dolce foco*), describing the paradox of amorous suffering and pleasure, is the phrase from which the title of this book is taken.

Notes to the "Di diversi a lei" *(exchange-sonnets)*

70. Lattanzio de Benucci (1521–1598) was a Sienese writer, diplomat, and legislator. He frequented the salons that Tullia held in her apartments. He is also one of the minor interlocutors in *Il Dialogo della Signora Tullia d'Aragona della infinità di amore* (*Dialogue on the Infinity of Love*).

71. "Battro" (now Balkh, known at one time as Bactria) is located in present-day northern Afghanistan. One of the world's oldest cities, it dates back to the third millennium B.C. In classical sources, Thule is an island in the far north, commonly used to mean a remote place beyond the boundaries of the known world. I have used "Kabul" instead of Bactria, however, as it is more familiar to contemporary readers.

72. The word "Tormi" is used in the original edition, but I have assumed it is a typographical error for "torni," the second-person singular, from *tornare* (to return).

73. A mountain in Boeotia, Greece, that is a sacred haunt of the Muses. See note 13 on Helicon in the introductory section and note 15 in the endnotes to the *Rime*.

74. See the sections featuring Muzio's prose, 91–98.

75. Alessandro Arrighi (d. 1581). According to biographical sources, Arrighi died in Rappallo en route to Genoa in the company of the Illustrious Signor Don Giovanni de' Medici. One of many in the family by that name, Alessandro was a Dominican priest. In line 8 of this poem, the reference is most likely to Glaucus, a mythical character who was changed into a god (cf. Ovid's *Metamorphoses*, Book XIII, lines 900–968).

76. A professional merchant, a writer, and a poet, Niccolò Martelli (1498–1555) was among the founders of the Accademia degli Umidi with his brother Ugolino.

See note 40. See also his letter comparing Tullia to Marco Tullio (Marcus Tullius) Cicero in Bongi, *Annali di Giolito*, 179, n. 1.

77. Arpino (Latin, *Arpinium*), in the Lazio region, is known as the birthplace of Cicero (106 B.C.–43 B.C.), the Roman statesman and author. In this poem, Martelli plays on the pun between Marcus Tullius (Marco *Tullio*) Cicero, and *Tullia*, a comparison he makes in a 1547 letter: "perchè se alhora fu un Tullio d'Arpino, hoggi è nel mondo una Tullia d'Aragona, che veramente si può dire honor secondo, a cui l'alma Poesia et la nobil Filosofia fanno un componimento celeste" (as [antiquity had] Tullio d'Arpino [Cicero], today the world has Tullia d'Aragona, of whom it truly can be said that honor follows her [...] joined by bountiful Poetry and noble Philosophy to make a celestial combination). (Bongi, *Annali di Giolito*, 179, n. 1). In a 1535 letter that appears with his translation of Cicero's *Pro Marcello*, Jacopo Nardi praises the Ciceronian eloquence of Tullia d'Aragona ("tulliana eloquenza"). Bongi, *Annali di Giolito*, 163. Translations mine.

78. *Anima*, the Latin word for soul, is used to mean the human capacity for reasoning. In Renaissance Italian poetry, sometimes the word *alma* is used as well.

79. As it is almost certain that this poem contains encoded references to the Accademia degli Umidi with which Martelli was associated, I have taken the liberty of substituting "Academy" for "umido crine." Its literal meaning is "moist hair" or "locks," evoking at once the poet's crown of laurel leaves, the Apollo and Daphne myth, and the name of the Accademia degli Umidi—of which Martelli was one of the founding members.

80. In one myth, Linus is a musician who taught Hercules; in another, he is the son of Apollo and Psamathe of Argos. His death inspires a lament known as the Linus song.

81. *Aliero* is the spelling used in the 1560 edition, most likely a typographical error; in keeping with the 1547 edition I have used *altero*, meaning high and proud.

82. Antonio Francesco Grazzini (1503–1583), also known as il Lasca, was a native of Florence, a founding member of the Accademia degli Umidi, later the Accademia Fiorentina, as well as the Accademia della Crusca (bran, or chaff). A satirist by nature, Grazzini often found himself at odds with the Florentine Academy in its stricter form under the authority of Cosimo de' Medici. For Grazzini's historical and cultural role in the Florentine court, see Zanrè, pages 59–78 and 87–89.

83. Regarding the isle of Thule, see note 71 above.

84. Ugolino Martelli (1519–1592) was one of the original founding members of the Umidi with authority in the Academy; a famous portrait of him was painted by Agnolo Bronzino. See Zanrè, especially 146–47, 154–56.

85. Smyrna is the former Greek name of the present-day Turkish city of Izmir. According to one legend, Homer was said to come from Smyrna; Virgil, of course, is from Mantua. A thousand pages written by either of them would be insufficient praise for Tullia, Martelli claims. Such hyperbolic praise is not uncommon in the period, but he is still exaggerating her virtues and eloquence, as she herself points out in the response-poem.

Notes to the Selected Prose

1. This preface appeared in the first edition of the *Dialogo della Signora Tullia d'Aragona della infinità di amore* (Venice: Giolito, 1547) as well as a later 1864 edition. It is reprinted in *Trattatisti del Cinquecento*, ed. Mario Pozzi (Bari: Laterza, 1978), 201.

2. In the philosophy of Plato (and his Neoplatonic followers), physical beauty is the bottom "rung" on the ladder of beauty, from which the soul is led upward toward true (spiritual) beauty.

3. That is, a metaphysical portrait, as opposed to a portrait that is seen using the human sense of sight. Like Augustine, Muzio holds spiritual "vision" to be superior.

4. In Latin, *ab eterno* means "from eternity."

5. In the original Italian, the word is *caduco*, from the Latin *caducus*, meaning fallen or inclined to fall; frail, perishable, and transitory.

6. See notes on Varchi (note 42, p. 115) and Benucci (note 70, p. 118), respectively.

7. Sperone Speroni's 1542 *Dialoghi d'amore* (written in 1537 and published in 1542), is a fictional conversation between Tullia and the poet Bernardo Tasso. See Sperone Speroni, *I Dialoghi di Messer Sperone Speroni*. (Venice: Aldus Manutius, 1542). See also Rinaldina Russell, "'Opinione' e 'giuoco' nel *Dialogo d'amore* di Sperone Speroni" in *La Parola del Testo: Semestrale di Filologia e Letteratura Italiana e Comparata dal Medioevo al Rinascimento*, Anno VI (2002), Fascicolo 1, 133–146.

8. Muzio writes of the classical "furor" which is most literally translated "ecstasy," the state of being "outside" or "beside" oneself. In classical thought, there are four types of "furor": Bacchic (inspired by wine or the god Bacchus), erotic (inspired by love, or Venus), poetic (inspired by the Muses or by Apollo), and prophetic (also inspired by Apollo).

9. Thalia is the muse of comedy, giving Tullia a more lighthearted and yet substantial poetic identity than that of the nymph Tirrhenia.

10. The abode of the Muses, which was sacred to Apollo.

11. Erato is the muse of epic poetry.

12. The fountain of Hippocrene (Greek, "horse spring") is on the slopes of Mount Helicon.

13. The heavens are divided into spheres, each having specific astrological and astronomical properties. Dante uses these words in a symbolic sense.

14. The Greek etymology is a bit far-fetched, but the Italian *verdeggiare* is from the Latin *viridis*, which includes the roots "vir" (man), and "virtù" (poetic skill). Here, Muzio is using an organic metaphor to describe poetic creation, and associates "Thalia" with the process.

15. The title is, "'A i Lettori' dell' *Meschino altramente detto il Guerrino* fatto in ottava rima dalla Tullia d'Aragona, opera, nella quale si veggono & intendono le parte principali di tutto il mondo, & molte altre dilettevolissime cose, da esser sommamente care ad ogni sorte di persona di bello ingegno." ('To the Readers' from 'The little wretched one also known as the little warrior,' a work in *ottava rima* by Tullia d'Aragona, in which the principal parts of the

world, and many other delightful things, to be held dear by all persons of distinguished wit.')

16. IIn the preface to his *Decameron*, Boccacio claims to be writing for the "solace" of women. Considering some of the stories (like "Patient Griselda"), some critics question this claim. Tullia d'Aragona expresses doubt as to whether Boccacio's *novelle* will be truly enjoyable to female readers. She objects to the portrayal of women in the *novelle* and epics of the time, which portray male fantasies of women and of courtesans. She might be employing irony: it is not so much that the works are unchaste as their authors purport to speak for women, in bad faith. See the Decameron Web URL: <http://www.stg.brown.edu/projects/decameron/engDecShowText.php?myID=proem&expand=>

17. Here, the metaphor of a poetic work "leav[ing] its form upon our memories" is similar to Dante's image of "recollecting" paradise: "Qual è colui che sognando vede, / che dopo 'l sogno la passione impressa / rimane, e altro a la mente non riede, cotal son io, che quasi tutta cessa / mia visione, ed ancor mi distilla nel core il dolce, che nacque da essa." (Like one who dreaming, sees, and after the dream the passion remains imprinted and nothing else comes to mind, such a one was I, my vision almost entirely ceased, yet in my heart is distilled the sweetness born from it.) *Paradiso*, XXXIII, 58–63.

18. Lodovico Dolce (1508–1568) is the editor of an edition of Dante's *Commedia*, printed in 1555 by Giolito (the publisher of Tullia, Muzio, and many of their friends). Although women were not "members" of the Academies, Tullia's salon was an alternative "academy," as Domenico Zanrè argues. See Zanrè, 147.

19. Girolamo Ruscelli (c. 1504–1566) was a Venetian cartographer, editor, and translator. He is perhaps best known for his Italian translation of Ptolemy's *Geography*.

20. See note 32 on Bembo, above, in the notes on the *Rime*.

21. Nanna and Pippa are characters in the sexually explicit *I Ragionamenti* by Pietro Aretino (1492–1556). *La Puttana errante* (the Errant Prostitute), has been attibuted to Lorenzo Venier but also to Aretino. The third book is probably *La Cazzaria* by Antonio Vignali, a burlesque satire of Sienese politics c. 1525. It has been translated into English by Ian Frederick Moulton as *The Book of the Prick* (Routledge, 2003). "*La Cazzaria* is raunchy, anti-clerical, misogynistic, elitist, parodic, and deeply invested in both Sienese politics and philosophical debates over proper objects of scholarly study through its shockingly obscene discussion of sex." William Stockton (review), "La Cazzaria: The Book of the Prick," *Journal for Early Modern Cultural Studies* 5, No. 2 (2005): 139–42.

22. Given the references to "Nanna" and "Pippa" in Pietro Aretino's *Ragionamenti*, the word *ragionamento* evokes not only the "discussion" of lascivious things, but also the text itself, the "dialogue" of an opportunistic prostitute and her daughter.

23. *Morgante Maggiore* (1483) by Luigi Pulci (1432–1484). See note 33 below.

24. [Regina] *Ancroia* (Queen Ancroia), a chivalric romance in verse, of anonymous authorship (Venice: G. B. et Melchior Sessa, 1499). The same publisher printed Tullia's epic *Il Meschino*.

25. Matteo Maria Boiardo's unfinished chivalric epic *Orlando Innamorato* (Venice:

Simone Bevilacqua, 1495), was used by Lodovico Ariosto as the basis for *Orlando Furioso*. Boiardo (c. 1441–1494) was a poet, a diplomat, a courtier at the Este court of Ferrara, as well as a translator of Herodotus, Xenophon, Lucian, and Apuleius.

26. Andrea da Barberino (b. ca. 1370), is the author of the prose narrative version of *Meschino decto Guerino*. Barberino's *I Reali di Francia* collection of Charlemagne legends is an entire book of *Buovo d'Antona*, an Italian version of *Sir Bevis*.

27. *Mambriano* (Venice, 1554). See also the *romanzo* (chivalric epic) by Cieco da Ferrara: *Libro d'arme e d'amore nomato Mambriano*, intro. and notes by Giuseppe Rua (Turin: Unione tipografico-editrice torinese, 1926). *Leandra* is another chivalric epic.

28. Lodovico Ariosto (1474–1533) was a Ferrarese nobleman and courtier, and the author of the extremely popular mock-chivalric epic *Orlando Furioso*, one of the most popular printed books of the Renaissance (first edition, 1516). After studying law, he dedicated himself to humanistic studies and writing literary works, such as *La Cassaria* (1508, not to be confused with *La Cazzaria*), *I suppositi* (1509), and other works. He was an ambassador for Pope Giulio II, Duke Alfonso I of Ferrara, and Pope Leo X.

29. This is probably the most revealing sentence in Tullia d'Aragona's writing, whether it is read tongue-in-cheek or straightforwardly. See the introduction to *Sweet Fire*, 14 and 18, for evidence as to how Tullia viewed the life into which she was born.

30. It is true that the source for *Il Meschino* is the Spanish prose narrative version of *Meschino decto Guerino*; however, the Italian translation by Andrea da Barberino probably was more accessible to Tullia d'Aragona than the original Spanish version.

31. The author implies that she is a person of judgment (*giudizio*), one of the most important literary criteria of the time.

32. In Pico della Mirandola's *Oration on the Dignity of Man*, free will determines one's place in the hierarchy of being, depending upon whether one's behavior is noble or base.

33. Luigi Pulci (1432–1484) became a protégé of Lorenzo de' Medici despite his humble origins. He is best known for his mock-chivalric epic *Morgante Maggiore* (1483). Just as Ariosto's *Orlando Furioso* recounts the adventures of Orlando, Pulci also narrates tales of the giant Morgante and his journeys to "pagan" lands.

34. In this passage, Tullia makes several important points, entering the linguistic and stylistic literary debates of her time. In the sixteenth century, the ultimate test of poetic skill was writing epic, not lyric poetry. With *Il Meschino*, Tullia achieves this goal; in the preface, she also expresses literary-critical ideas *about* epic poetry. For example, her reference to the *via mezzana* ("middle way") is a direct refutation of the elitist position of *literati* such as Pietro Bembo and Giraldi Cinthio. Giraldi, an personal enemy of Tullia's, wrote a treatise on the *romanzo*, a discourse on tragedy, and tragic dramas with classical themes (e.g., *Orbecche* and *Canace*). His treatise is concerned with the proper uses of classicism in Cinquecento poetry. He also wrote a rather unsuccessful epic in *ottava rima*

entitled *dell'Ercole*. Pietro Bembo, in his *Prose della lingua volgare*, argues for Tuscan as the *lingua franca* of Italian literature. Defiantly, Tullia attributes value to dialects other than Tuscan. She also draws from classical sources, using the Horatian criteria of *dulce* and *utile* (pleasure *and* delight). Her arguments for the "middle way" and to use "the language of all Italy" imply an unusual conception of an audience of common readers—an audience in which she specifically includes women. Not only unusual but courageously iconoclastic, these ideas pose an alternative to the high culture represented by Giraldi, Bembo, Tasso, and other contemporary writers of the era. Furthermore, Tullia d'Aragona is the first woman to write a work of such magnitude in the *romanzo* genre.

Selected Bibliography

Alighieri, Dante. *La divina commedia*. Ed. Giuseppe Villaroel, introduction by Eugenio Montale. 3 vols. Milan: Mondadori, 1985.

Allaire, Gloria. "Tullia d'Aragona's *Il Meschino* as Key to a Reappraisal of Her Work." *Quaderni d'Italianistica* 16, No. 1 (1995): 33–50.

d'Aragona, Tullia. *Dialogo della Signora Tullia d'Aragona della infinità di amore*. In *Trattatisti del Cinquecento*, ed. Mario Pozzi. Bari: G. Laterza, 1978.

———. *Dialogue on the Infinity of Love*. Ed. and trans. Rinaldina Russell and Bruce Merry. With introduction and notes by Rinaldina Russell. Part of the series The Other Voice in Early Modern Europe, series eds. Margaret L. King and Albert Rabil, Jr. Chicago: University of Chicago Press, 1997.

———. *Il Meschino altramente detto il Guerrino*. Venice: G. B. et Melchior Sessa, 1560.

———. *Rime della Signora Tullia di Aragona et di diversi a lei*. Venice: Gabriel Giolito de Ferrari et Fratelli, 1547; 1549. Reprint *Rime della Signora Tullia di Aragona et di diversi a lei. Nuovamente corrette e ristampate*. Venice: Gabriel Giolito de Ferrari et Fratelli, 1560.

———. *Rime della Signora Tullia di Aragona et di diversi a lei*. Naples: Presso Antonio Bulifon, 1693.

———. *Rime della Signora Tullia d'Aragona, cortigiana del secolo XVI*. Ed. Enrico Celani. Bologna: Editrice Forni di Bologna, 1891; Reprint, Bologna: Commissione per i testi di lingua, 1968.

Aretino, Pietro. *Aretino's Dialogues*. Preface + trans. by Raymond Rosenthal. Epilogue by Margaret F. Rosenthal. New York: Marsilio Books, 1994.

———. *Sei giornate*. Ed. Giovanni Aquilecchia. Rome: G. Laterza, 1969; 1980.

Bassanese, Fiora. "Private Lives and Public Lies: Texts by Courtesans of the Italian Renaissance." *Texas Studies in Language and Literature* 30 (1988): 295–319.

Bausi, Francesco. "Le rime di e per Tullia d'Aragona." In *Les femmes écrivains en Italie au Moyen Age et à la Renaissance*. Aix-en-Provence: Université de Provence, 1994.

Bembo, Pietro. *Prose e Rime*. Ed. Carlo Dionisotti. Turin: Unione tipografico-editrice torinese, 1966.

Benedetti, Laura, Julia L. Hairston, and Silvia Ross, eds. *Gendered Contexts: New Perspectives in Italian Cultural Studies*. New York: Peter Lang, 1996.

Benson, Pamela Joseph. *The Invention of the Renaissance Woman: The Challenge of Female Independence in the Literature and Thought of Italy and England*. University Park, PA: Pennsylvania State University Press, 1992.

Biagi, Guido. "Un'etèra romana. Tullia d'Aragona." *Nuova antologia*, series III, 4, No. 16 (1886): 655–711. Reprinted with revisions as "Tullia d'Aragona." In *Fiorenza*, *fior che sempre rinnovella: quadri e figure di vita fiorentina*, 137-261. Florence: Battistelli, 1925.

Bongi, Salvatore. "Rime della Signora Tullia di Aragona et di diversi a lei." In *Annali di Gabriel Giolito de' Ferrari*. Vol. 1, 150-99. Rome: Presso i Principali Librai, 1890.

Brackett, J. K. "The Florentine Onestà and the Control of Prostitution, 1403–1680," *Sixteenth Century Journal* 24, No. 2 (1993), 273–300.

Braden, Gordon. *Petrarchan Love and the Continental Renaissance*. New Haven: Yale University Press, 1999.

Buranello, Robert. *"Figura meretricis*: Tullia d'Aragona in Sperone Speroni's *Dialogo di amore." Spunti e ricerche* 15 (2000): 53–68.

Chastel, Andre. *Luigi d'Aragona: Un cardinale del Rinascimento in viaggio per l'Europa.* Bari: Laterza, 1995.

Cox, Virginia. *The Renaissance Dialogue: Literary Dialogue in its Social and Political Contexts, Castiglione to Galileo.* Cambridge: Cambridge University Press, 1992.

Eisenbichler, Konrad, Review, Dialogue on the Infinity of Love, *Sixteenth Century Journal,* XXIX, No. 2 (1998): 611–12.

————, ed. *The Cultural Politics of Duke Cosimo I de' Medici.* Aldershot, England; Burlington, VT: Ashgate, 2001.

————. *The Cultural World of Eleonora di Toledo: Duchess of Florence and Siena.* Aldershot, England; Burlington, VT: Ashgate, 2004.

Ferroni, Giulio. *Poesia del Cinquecento.* Milan: Garzanti, 1978.

Freccero, John. "The Fig Tree and the Laurel: Petrarch's Poetics." *Diacritics* 5 (1975): 35–40.

Giraldi, Giambattista Cinzio. *De gli Hecatommith[i] di M. Giovanbattista Gyraldi Cinthio.* Nel Monte Regale: Appresso Lionardo Torrentino, 1565; *Gli Ecatommiti, ovvero cento novelle di G. B. Cintio.* Turin: Pomba, 1953.

Greene, Roland Arthur. *Post-Petrarchism: Origins and Innovations of the Western Lyric Sequence.* Princeton: Princeton University Press, 1991.

Greene, Thomas M. *The Light in Troy: Imitation and Discovery in Renaissance Poetics.* New Haven: Yale University Press, 1982.

Grendler, Paul F. *Schooling in Renaissance Italy: Literacy and Learning 1300–1600.* In The Johns Hopkins University Studies in Historical and Political Science, 107th series, No. 1. Baltimore and London: The Johns Hopkins University Press, 1989.

Hairston, Julia L. "Out of the Archive: Four Newly-Identified Figures in Tullia d'Aragona's *Rime della Signora Tullia di Aragona et di diversi a lei* (1547)." *Modern Language Notes* 118, No. 1 (2003): 257–63.

————. "Tullia d'Aragona, ca. 1510–1556." http://www.lib.uchicago.edu/efts/IWW/BIOS/A0004.html.

Jones, Ann Rosalind. *The Currency of Eros: Women's Love Lyric in Europe, 1540–1620.* Bloomington: Indiana University Press, 1990.

————. "New Songs for the Swallow: Ovid's Philomela in Tullia d'Aragona and Gaspara Stampa." In *Refiguring Woman: Perspectives on Gender and the Italian Renaissance.* Marilyn Migiel and Juliana Schiesari, eds., 263–77. Ithaca: Cornell University Press, 1991.

Jordan, Constance. "Listening to the Other Voice in Early Modern Europe." *Renaissance Quarterly*, LI, No. 5 (1998): 188.

Kirkham, Victoria, and Pamela Joseph Benson, eds. *Strong Voices, Weak History: Early Women Writers & Canons in England, France, & Italy.* Ann Arbor: University of Michigan Press, 2005.

MacLean, Ian. *The Renaissance Notion of Woman: A Study in the Fortunes of Scholasticism and Medical Science in European Intellectual Life.* Cambridge and New York: Cambridge University Press, 1990.

Masson, Georgina. *Courtesans of the Italian Renaissance.* New York: St. Martin's Press, 1975. Also printed in London: Secker and Warburg, 1975.

Migiel, Marilyn, and Juliana Schiesari, eds. *Refiguring Woman: Perspectives on Gender and the Italian Renaissance.* Ithaca: Cornell University Press, 1991.

Muzio, Girolamo. *Lettere, 137v–139v.* Ristampa anastatica dell' edizione Sermartelli, 1590. Ed. Luciana Borsetto. Ferrara: Sala Bolognese, 1985.

Pallitto, Elizabeth A. "Apocalypse and/or Metamorphosis: Chronographia and Topographia in Petrarch's XXII & Tullia d'Aragona's LV." *Comitatus: Journal of Medieval & Renaissance Studies,* No. 33 (2002), 59–76.

————. "Translations of Four Poems by Tullia d'Aragona." *Forum Italicum* 36, No. 1 (Spring 2002), 179–89.

Panizza, Letizia, ed. *Women in Italian Renaissance Culture and Society.* Legenda Series. Oxford: European Humanities Research Center, 2000.

Petrarca, Francesco. *Canzoniere.* Ed. Piero Cudini. Milan: Garzanti, 1994.

————. *Petrarch's Lyric Poems: The Rime Sparse and Other Lyrics.* Ed. Robert M. Durling. Cambridge, MA: Harvard University Press, 1976.

Rosenthal, Margaret. *The Honest Courtesan.* Chicago and London: University of Chicago Press, 1992.

Russell, Rinaldina, ed. *Feminist Encyclopedia of Italian Literature.* Westport, CT: Greenwood Press, 1997.

————, ed. *Italian Women Writers: A Bio-bibliographical Sourcebook.* Westport, CT: Greenwood Press, 1994.

————. "'Opinione' e 'giuoco' nel *Dialogo d'amore* di Sperone Speroni." In *La Parola del Testo: Semestrale di Filologia e Letteratura Italiana e Comparata dal Medioevo al Rinascimento.* Anno VI (2002), Fascicolo 1, 133-146.

Samuels, Richard S. "Benedetto Varchi, the Accademia degli Infiammati, and the Origins of the Italian Academic Movement." *Renaissance Quarterly* 29, No. 4 (1976): 599–634.

Smarr, Janet Levarie. "A Dialogue of Dialogues: Tullia d'Aragona and Sperone Speroni." *Modern Language Notes* 113 (1998): 204–12.

————. "Substituting for Laura: Objects of Desire for Renaissance Women Poets." *Comparative Literature Studies* 28, No. 1 (Winter 2001).

Speroni, Sperone. *I Dialoghi di Messer Sperone Speroni.* Venice: Aldus Manutius, 1542.

Stortoni, Laura Anna. *Women Poets of the Renaissance: Courtly Ladies and Courtesans.* Trans. Laura Anna Stortoni and Mary Prentice Lillie. New York: Italica Press, 1997.

Varchi, Benedetto. *Opere di Benedetto Varchi*. Vol. 2, 289a, 655, 657b–685a. Trieste: Sezione letterario-artistica del Lloyd Austriaco, 1859.

Vitiello, Justin. "Gaspara Stampa: The Ambiguities of Martyrdom." *Modern Language Notes* 90 (1975): 58–71.

———. "A Selection of Medieval and Renaissance Italian Love Poems." *Forum Italicum* 29, No. 2 (Fall 1995): 382–90.

Zanrè, Domenico. *Cultural Non-Conformity in Early Modern Florence*. Aldershot, England; Burlington, VT: Ashgate, 2004.